Day by Day
with People of the Bible

Day by Day
with People of the Bible

Reflections for Teens

Dennis Kurtz
Michaela Hedican, OSB
Judy Kramer, OSB
with contributions by Virginia Halbur

Saint Mary's Press®

The publishing team included Virginia Halbur, development editor; Brian Singer-Towns, co-editor; Lorraine Kilmartin, reviewer; cover image © 2005 Daniel Speck, FreeStockPhotos.com; prepress and manufacturing coordinated by the production departments of Saint Mary's Press.

Printed in the United States of America

4325

ISBN 978-0-88489-922-8

Library of Congress Cataloging-in-Publication Data

Kurtz, Dennis.
   Day by day with people of the Bible : reflections for teens / Dennis Kurtz, Michaela Hedican, Judy Kramer ; with contributions by Virginia Halbur.
      p. cm.
ISBN 978-0-88489-922-8 (pbk.)
   1. Christian teenagers—Prayers and devotions. 2. Bible—Meditations. 3. Devotional calendars. I. Hedican, Michaela. II. Kramer, Judy, 1939- III. Halbur, Virginia. IV. Title.

BV4531.3.K87 2007
242'.63—dc22

                                                    2007004459

Adam and Eve: God's Best

> God saw everything that he had made, and indeed,
> it was very good.
>
> (Genesis 1:31)

After God finished creating the world, he found it to
be **very** good. Human beings were the culmination of
creation, made in God's image and likeness. So we too
are **very** good.

There is no better feeling than when you have created
something wonderful with your own hands. You feel good
because it is the culmination of all the best in you. You sit
back and in honest review admire what you have brought
into being. You have a special affinity for this creation.
Now take that feeling and multiply it many times over,
and you will begin to recognize how God feels toward
creation.

When have you been pleased with what you have
created because it was good? How has your own
creativity helped you to understand God as Creator?

> *Creator God, thank you for creating me as a uniquely
> wonderful person and for giving me the ability to
> cocreate with you.*

• To go deeper: Read Genesis 1:14–31.

Adam and Eve: Companions in Life

> And the rib that the LORD God had taken from the man he made into a woman.
>
> (Genesis 2:22)

What a wonderful blessing to have a trusted friend. Life is full of so many things, good and not so good, that we want to share with one another. God understood this about human beings, so God created Adam and Eve as equal companions, derived from the same flesh.

As a Triune God, Father, Son, and Holy Spirit coexist as a community in mutual love. The love within the Trinity serves as a model for how we are to love one another. In God's plan, mutual love is the basis of marriage. This is symbolized by God taking an inner part of Adam and miraculously expanding it into a whole person. God brings together two individuals who, being of one flesh, are perfectly matched.

Do you have a friend with whom you can share the intimate details of your life experiences?

God, you know me from the inside out. Give me people in my life who can know me in a similar way.

- To go deeper: Read Genesis 2:18–24.

Adam and Eve: God Provides

And the LORD God planted a garden in Eden, in the east.

(Genesis 2:8)

After creating Adam, God planted a garden for him and provided for Adam's every need, even to the point of creating a human companion for him. The garden provided food for them and a place for them to nurture their relationship with each other and with God. Adam and Eve were given the task of cultivating and caring for the garden. In God's design, human beings share responsibility with God in caring for all creation.

Today it is critically important to remember that God has charged us with caring for the world. With so many forces threatening our environment, we all need to do our part to care for the earth.

When have you felt in complete harmony with all of God's creation? How do you demonstrate care for the earth?

Thank you, God, for generously providing me with everything I need to sustain my life. May I always express my gratitude through kindness to others and care for the earth.

• To go deeper: Read Genesis 1:8–15.

Eve: Desiring False Wisdom

> God commanded . . . "You may freely eat of every tree of the garden; but of the tree of the knowledge of good and evil you shall not eat."
>
> (Genesis 2:16–17)

Despite God's warning, Eve fell for the serpent's temptation that she could be equal to God in wisdom if only she would eat the forbidden fruit. She was seduced into thinking she would be happier if she had more than she already possessed. But instead of gaining more, Adam and Eve lost their perfect life. What a shocking reality. They lost their innocence and could never again look upon life the same way.

Have you ever wanted more—influence, friends, clothes, electronics—when you already have enough? Marketers work hard to convince you that you need their products for true happiness!

Which particular things in your culture lure you with the empty promise of providing fulfillment?

Merciful God, you are always by my side, even when I allow myself to be deceived by others. Give me your grace so I will have the confidence to turn back to you.

- To go deeper: Read Genesis 3:1–13.

Adam and Eve: Held Accountable

"By the sweat of your face you shall eat bread."

(Genesis 3:19)

Adam and Eve were banished from the Garden of Eden because of the seriousness of their offense. To survive, they now had to work hard for what was once easily attainable. Whenever trust is violated and relationships are broken, the road to repairing them is usually long and intense. One hope remained for Adam and Eve—that God would continue to offer his unconditional love to them.

We all have experienced the painful consequences of making a bad decision. Bad decisions not only cause us to suffer but also can impact others in a significant way. We are responsible for the consequences of our actions, whether for good or bad.

What are some harsh consequences you have had to face because of your own bad decisions? Where did you find hope in the situation?

God, I know you are always there for me even when I feel thousands of miles away from you. Continue to sustain me in your love.

- To go deeper: Read Genesis 3:14–24.

Cain and Abel: The Two Faces of Humanity

"If you do well, will you not be accepted? And if you do not do well, sin is lurking at the door, its desire is for you, but you must master it."

(Genesis 4:7)

Human nature is complex. Each person can become a Cain or an Abel, choosing to act in a way that is good or bad. The Scriptures tell us that human beings are not subjects (slaves) of sin, but rather we can triumph over sin. It is a matter of desire.

Sometimes when we hear someone has done something bad, we debate whether the root cause was nurture or nature. In other words, was the person born evil, or did something in his or her upbringing make him or her evil? The story of Cain and Abel tells us that no one is destined for evil. God has given every person the ability to choose one or the other.

Have you had to choose between good and evil actions in your life? What is your compelling desire?

God, in your infinite wisdom, you gifted me with free choice. May I always use it to choose good in life.

• To go deeper: Read Genesis 4:1–16.

Introduction

The Bible recounts the stories of many people of faith who throughout salvation history have put their trust in God. In a real way, these people are our spiritual ancestors, who show us how to deepen our relationship with God. *Day by Day with People of the Bible* looks at the lives of over seventy biblical characters. These people were chosen because they play an important role in salvation history. Generally, each person or family is covered by a series of seven reflections. The first day of the series usually begins with a brief background on the biblical person or persons covered in the series. The six reflections that follow focus on a particular aspect of the person's or people's life. In an effort to tie in with the liturgical calendar, reflections on the biblical characters are not necessarily in chronological order.

Each daily entry begins with a Scripture passage related to the biblical person's story, followed by a reflection on that passage that speaks to the experience of the biblical person and how her or his situation relates to your own life. The reflection may provide historical or cultural background, theological insights, or aspects of Church teaching to deepen your understanding of the context in which the biblical person's story was written or the story's meaning for your life today. A brief question and prayer are provided after the reflection to help you integrate what you have learned into your daily life. The

"To go deeper" section at the end of each reflection lists suggested Scripture readings for further study.

Try to spend ten to fifteen minutes each day with the reflections in order to understand how God is calling you to deepen your faith and share the message of God's love with others. To facilitate this process, you may wish to start a journal in which you write your responses to each day's question.

It is our hope that through these daily reflections, you will not only grow in your knowledge of the people God has called throughout history but you will also see parallels between their story and your own life experiences. God uses ordinary human experiences to nurture faith in each of us.

Cain and Seth: The Population of the Earth

> "Cain knew his wife and she conceived and bore Enoch."
>
> (Genesis 4:17)

> "[Adam] became the father of a son in his likeness, according to his image, and named him Seth."
>
> (Genesis 5:3)

Just as Cain chose evil, so did his descendants. Lamech had a man killed for wounding him, and a teenager killed for striking him. Cain's descendants lived by a law of extreme retaliation. But revenge does not solve anything and only perpetuates the cycle of violence. This tendency to want to retaliate remains a part of the human condition today. An alternative, however, is found in the person of Seth. Seth, according to legend, was a good and righteous man, and his descendants produced Noah, the archetype of a good and righteous person.

Can you think of a time when you asked for justice for some harm done to you when what you really wanted was revenge?

God of justice and fairness, help me seek your justice rather than revenge in all situations in my life.

- To go deeper: Read Genesis 4:17—5:32.

Noah: Am I the Only One?

> The Lord saw that the wickedness of humankind
> was great. . . . But Noah found favor in the sight
> of the Lord.
>
> (Genesis 6:5,8)

As the mythical story of Noah begins, all other human beings have been led astray and only Noah is found to be faithful. God decides to destroy all creation and then asks Noah to do something strange—to build a three-story houseboat to save his family and a pair of every living creature. God entrusts Noah with a strange and difficult task. People thought Noah was delusional, but Noah carried out God's command even though he must have felt foolish and alone. Early theologians compared Noah's ark to the Church: both try to carry all sorts of characters through a dangerous life to safety!

How do you respond when you think you are the only one being asked to do something—such as observe a curfew, help with household chores, or attend church?

Dear God, help me be courageous and respond faithfully when I am asked to do something difficult.

• To go deeper: Read Genesis 6:5–17.

Noah: God Makes a Promise

"I will establish my covenant with you."

(Genesis 6:18)

The first time we find the term *covenant* in the Scriptures is in the Book of Genesis. God speaks with Noah and promises to be in covenant with him. A covenant is a solemn and firm promise made between human beings or between God and human beings. God was terribly disappointed with the wickedness of people. But through faithful Noah, God decided to give the human race another chance.

If you have ever been deeply hurt by someone, you know how difficult it is to forgive and trust that person again. We should remember God's covenant with Noah. Despite the hurt human sin causes, God is always ready to give us another chance. Can we be as forgiving?

Have you ever been given a second chance? What promises did you make as a result of that second chance?

God of second chances, thanks for giving me another chance when I fail, and help me always be faithful to you.

- To go deeper: Read Genesis 6:18–20.

Noah: His Unnamed Wife

> And Noah with his sons and his wife and his sons'
> wives went into the ark to escape the waters of the
> flood.
>
> (Genesis 7:7)

Noah's wife certainly was a vital partner in saving the human race and all the species of animals on the earth. However, we do not even have a name for this courageous woman. Because most of the Scriptures were written by men, even heroic women who followed God with great faith are seldom recorded or named in the Bible.

Noah's wife must have loved Noah with every fiber of her being in order to believe and trust in God as her husband did. Build an ark? Get everyone and animals on board? The uncertainty, the dreadful voyage to an unknown landing, the discomfort and danger of the trip must have been terrible!

What name would you give to Noah's wife?

Who are the female unnamed heroes you know? What can you do to recognize their contributions?

Dear God, bless the women who are models of courage and faith for me, and help me serve as a model for others.

- To go deeper: Read Genesis 7:6–17.

Noah: The Flood

> And the waters increased, and bore up the ark, and
> it rose high above the earth.
>
> (Genesis 7:17)

Noah had done everything God had commanded. The huge boat was ready. Noah warned and gathered his family. The animals were waiting to board. What squealing, shouting, cursing, and doubting! Then they heard the first clap of thunder. The forty days and nights that followed were full of uncertainty and terror. Noah and his family saw God's power and might. The rain poured down, soaking, choking, and drowning all in its path.

Endings and new beginnings are rarely easy, especially when we are victims of circumstances beyond our control. These times really test our faith in God.

Have you ever experienced an unexpected move, a dramatic loss, or the sudden death of someone? Where was God for you during this time?

God of justice and love, lift me and carry me over the troubled waters of my life. Wash away all that is displeasing to you and give me a new start.

• To go deeper: Read Genesis 7:17–24.

Noah: Safe at Last

> In the seventh month, on the seventeenth day of the
> month, the ark came to rest on the mountains of
> Ararat.
>
> (Genesis 8:4)

Calculating time and distance has developed into a
sophisticated science in our modern world. But Noah and
his family measured their journey far more simply. When
the ark's motion (and no doubt motion sickness) stopped,
they needed a way to know if their terrifying journey was
at an end.

So Noah sent out a raven and later a dove to search
for dry ground in the early weeks after the ark came to rest.
Finally, the dove brought back an olive branch. Safety at
last! The promise of a better future, a new start, spread
before them. Hope was born again that day.

What signs of hope do you see in our world today?

*Symbols of white doves and two fingers lifted in
a peace gesture are only a start, Lord. Let us see
progress toward peace in our lifetime.*

• To go deeper: Read Genesis 8:1–18.

Noah: The Rainbow Promise

> The LORD said, ". . . I will never again curse the ground because of humankind, . . . nor will I ever again destroy every living creature as I have done. . . . When the [rainbow] is in the clouds, I will see it and remember the everlasting covenant between God and every living creature."
>
> (Genesis 8:21, 9:16)

The first thing Noah and his family did after they safely climbed out of the ark was to offer a sacrifice to God. God responded to that pleasing gift with a sign—a rainbow in the sky. The rainbow never fails to enchant us and fill us with awe. The rainbow is a sign of the covenant God made with Noah (and with us all) to never again destroy the whole earth. The promise we make in Baptism—to believe and to turn away from evil—is our covenant response.

When did you last see a rainbow and marvel at the hope it stands for? How are you a sign of hope for others?

God of goodness, beauty, and glory, help me live out my baptismal promise to be a sign of hope for others.

• To go deeper: Read Genesis 8:20—9:17.

Noah: Noah's Boys

> The sons of Noah who went out of the ark were Shem, Ham, and Japheth.
>
> (Genesis 9:18)

Noah's boys had to get along while they were afloat, but once on dry land, discord began. The brothers parted, headed in three different directions, settled the land, and fathered people of many cultures and languages. Shem and his family settled in the hill country to the east. Ham, the second son of Noah, became leader of a mighty clan of hunters. However, Ham's son, Canaan, dishonored his grandfather and was cursed and disowned by Noah. The third son, Japheth, settled along the coast, and his kin became prosperous merchants.

The author of Genesis used this story to explain why the people of his time were often in conflict. Although we are all part of the same human family, true peace escapes us.

What are some causes of division in your own family? Are you a peacemaker? What does it take to be a peacemaker?

Lord God of goodness, help me respect and trust others so that one day I will attain lasting peace.

- To go deeper: Read Genesis 9:18–28.

Abram: Moving On Out

The Lord said to Abram, "Go from your country and
your kindred and your father's house to the land that
I will show you. I will make of you a great nation,
and I will bless you."

(Genesis 12:1–2)

The most growth-filled experiences in life often are the
result of our ability to take risks and trust that all will be
well. Abram—the father in faith of Jews, Christians, and
Muslims—found this to be true in his life. For God's blessing
to be fulfilled, Abram had to leave behind his comfortable
and familiar life and allow God to lead him into a new
land with new experiences.

Young peoples' lives are full of challenges and the
unknown—taking new classes, starting new jobs, meeting
new people. Life is full of opportunities that require us to
trust that God will show us the way as we journey.

As your life unfolds, what new experiences require you
to trust in God?

*Guide me, Lord, as I am called to enter new areas in
my life. May I trust you to bless all my ventures.*

• To go deeper: Read Genesis 12:1–9.

Abram: Too Much Stuff

Abram was very rich in livestock, in silver, and in gold. . . . Now Lot [Abraham's nephew], who went with Abram, also had flocks and herds and tents, so that the land could not support both of them living together.

(Genesis 13:2,5–6)

As Abram and his nephew Lot discovered, having more possessions doesn't necessarily lead to peace and security. There was a limit to what the land would support.

Having the best and the latest of everything is sometimes a goal of young people today. The North American ideal seems to be one of ever-growing affluence. You may find, however, that all these possessions lead to conflicts and quarrels. And it may actually lead to an unfair distribution of the earth's resources. Finding just and peaceful ways to share God's gifts continues to be a challenge.

When have possessions been a source of conflict between you and a friend or family member? How did you resolve it?

Giver of all good gifts, help me realize that my possessions are meant to be used in the service of others.

• To go deeper: Read Genesis 13:1–12.

Abram: A Star-Spangled Promise

> [The LORD] brought him outside and said, "Look toward heaven and count the stars, if you are able to count them." Then he said to [Abram], "So shall your descendants be."
>
> (Genesis 15:5)

Stars are an ancient and universal symbol of dreams, hopes, and desires; in fact, the word *desire* means "of the stars." Abram desired an heir, and God affirmed his desire by pointing to the stars. By that simple gesture, Abram was convinced God's word could be trusted.

You might sometimes feel that living as a Christian is pointless and impossible. We see Christian people acting hypocritically, sometimes even Church leaders' not living up to their responsibility. When those times happen, look at the stars and remember that our trust is in God's word and not in fallible human beings.

Which of God's promises are most difficult for you to believe?

Creator of the stars of night, light my way when I am in the darkness of doubt.

• To go deeper: Read Genesis 15:1–20.

Abram: What's in a Name?

Then Abram fell on his face; and God said to him,
". . . No longer shall your name be Abram, but
your name shall be Abraham; for I have made you
the ancestor of a multitude of nations."

(Genesis 17:3,5)

Children often protect themselves from insults by singing,
"Sticks and stones can break my bones, but names
can never hurt me." A change in name can, however,
signify a turning point in one's life. Many people prefer to
drop a childhood nickname as they move into the more
sophisticated teenage years. You may even ask others
to call you by a variation of your name that has special
meaning for you.

Whatever our situation, a special name we've been
given by loved ones unites us to them in a particular way.
Like Abraham, we know we are lovingly cared for every
time we hear our special name.

What special names have loved ones given you?

*Loving God, as you call me by name, may I respond
in faith and trust in your word.*

• To go deeper: Read Genesis 17:1–27.

Abram: Taking in Strangers

> He looked up and saw three men standing near him. When he saw them, he ran from the tent entrance to meet them, and bowed down to the ground. He said, "My lord, if I find favor with you, do not pass by your servant."
>
> (Genesis 18:2–3)

Encountering a new student in the halls of school or on the athletic field often feels awkward. What should you say or do? Abraham, our father in faith, sets before us an inspiring example of welcoming a stranger. Like Abraham, we are to go out of our way to greet and welcome the new student and the stranger.

People are often afraid of strangers. It can take real courage to reach out to someone you don't know. In the end, Abraham discovered that strangers are God's messengers. We too may be surprised by the blessings we receive from the new people we welcome into our lives.

When were you a stranger in an unfamiliar setting? What did it feel like?

Welcoming God, hear my prayer of thanks for all who have made me feel welcome in new situations in my life.

• To go deeper: Read Genesis 18:1–8.

Abraham: Isaac, "Son of Laughter"

> Sarah conceived and bore Abraham a son in his old age, at the time of which God had spoken to him. Abraham gave the name Isaac to his son whom Sarah bore him.
>
> (Genesis 21:2–3)

Old age seemed to provide no hindrance to God's desire to fulfill a promise. Both Abraham and his wife, Sarah, were beyond their childbearing years. Upon hearing the promise of a son, they both laughed. Isaac's name, "son of laughter," was a permanent reminder that God sometimes has the last laugh. Do you believe God enjoys a good laugh and likes to surprise us at times? Does God take delight in your times of good fun with friends?

Are you able to gently laugh at yourself when you think God can't possibly see you through a tough time?

Teach me, Lord, to delight in the joy of laughter and to realize it is a gift from you.

• To go deeper: Read Genesis 21:1–8.

Abraham: Tested to the Limits

> After these things God tested Abraham. He said to him, "Abraham!" And he said, "Here I am." [God] said, "Take your son, your only son Isaac, whom you love, and go to the land of Moriah, and offer him there as a burnt offering on one of the mountains that I shall show you."
>
> (Genesis 22:1–2)

Tests of any kind tend to bring with them feelings of anxiety and dread. God's request of Abraham seemed to be the ultimate test of willingness to do whatever God asked. Abraham was determined to give anything, even his beloved son Isaac.

Abraham's faith in God amid his test is an encouragement to us. At times, we really believe we are doing God's will, but then our hopes are dashed or our plans seem to fail. We shouldn't lose faith during those times, but we should keep listening for God's voice and direction as Abraham did.

When have you felt God's putting you "to the test"?

Grant me the courage I need, Lord, to lovingly respond, "Ready!" to your will for my life.

• To go deeper: Read Genesis 22:1–14.

Sarah: Mother of Our Faith

> "[God] will bless [Sarah], and she shall give rise to nations; kings of peoples shall come from her."
>
> (Genesis 17:16)

Sarah was the wife of Abraham and the mother of Isaac, thus the mother of the Hebrew people. Sarah's father-in-law, Terah, decided to move with his family from Ur, which today is southern Iraq, to Canaan in the hope of finding a better life in a new land. As a woman of that time, Sarah would not have had much say in this decision.

Yet we know that Sarah placed her trust in God throughout her life and set forth on an adventure of faith that granted her a distinguished place in the biblical story. As a young person, you may not always feel that you have a say in all the decisions affecting you. Like Sarah, you need to place your trust in God.

When have you placed complete trust in God? How has trusting God led to new opportunities and a deeper journey into the heart of God?

Mother Sarah, continue to show me the way to faith by helping me place my trust in God.

- To go deeper: Read Genesis 11:31 — 12:9.

Sarah: God's Future Promise

> Your wife Sarah shall bear you a son, and you shall name him Isaac.
>
> (Genesis 17:19)

The name Sarah means "princess." God chose Sarah for a significant role in the salvation of humankind. The mother of Isaac and of the Hebrew people, she is also our mother in faith. It was through the faith of Abraham and Sarah that the foundation of the Jewish and Christian faiths was formed. Jews and Christians today profess a belief in one God, Creator of all.

Do you ever wonder what fruits your faith will produce in the future? It is difficult to imagine that being faithful to God now may have positive results in the future. Sarah could not have known that we today would hold her in high esteem because of her conscious act of being faithful to God.

We are all chosen by God for a special role in passing on the faith. What is God calling you to?

Sarah, help me as I discern the special role God wishes me to fulfill.

- To go deeper: Read Genesis 17:15–22.

Sarah: Questioning God's Promise

[Abraham's] wife bore him no children.

(Genesis 16:1)

Sarah knew God to be true to his word. God promised that a great nation would come from Sarah and Abraham—that their descendants would number more than the stars in the sky or the sands of the seashore. As Sarah and Abraham grew older, even though in faith they believed God's promise could be fulfilled, their humanness led them to question: How was it physically possible to have children when they were past childbearing age?

Do you sometimes doubt your God-given potential? Even though you believe that in God all things are possible, do you sometimes question whether God is actually working in your life? It is human to wonder if you can fulfill all that God is asking of you!

What human limitations do you have that cause you to question your God-given potential?

In my doubting, mother Sarah, help me remember that in God all things are possible.

• To go deeper: Read Genesis 15:1–6.

Sarah: In God's Own Time

> [Sarah] said to [Abraham], "You see that the LORD has prevented me from bearing children."
>
> (Genesis 16:2)

When Sarah determined she was too old to give birth to any children, she decided to help God keep his promise. As was the acceptable custom, Sarah gave Abraham permission to have a child with her maidservant Hagar. With Sarah's blessing, Abraham took Hagar as his wife and had a son named Ishmael. God blessed Ishmael greatly, but God was still intent on fulfilling the promise of a great nation coming through Sarah.

Part of being human is feeling impatient as we wait for the fulfillment of promises made to us. Future rewards are difficult to wait for because we want to experience them sooner rather than later. However, God's promises to us will be fulfilled in God's own time—we just have to be patient.

What future promise do you wish would be fulfilled in your life today?

God, be patient with me when I find it difficult to wait for your promises to be fulfilled.

- To go deeper: Read Genesis 16:1–4.

Sarah: Laughter of Disbelief

So Sarah laughed to herself.

(Genesis 18:12)

Sarah overheard the conversation between Abraham and the three strangers that had visited them. The strangers told Sarah's husband that at this time next year, when they returned, Sarah will have given birth to a son. Because of Sarah's advanced age, she laughed in disbelief at this prediction. Sarah laughed to herself, but the strangers, who were messengers of God, were informed by God of Sarah's laughter. When Sarah was confronted, out of fear she denied she had laughed.

God knows us like a best friend—one who knows what we are thinking, even though we do not express our thoughts in words. God is a friend who understands our moments of disbelief and who seeks to bring us to understanding.

What unexpected thing might God bring to life in you?

God, you know me better than I know myself. Continue to reveal yourself to me.

- To go deeper: Read Genesis 18:1–15.

Sarah: Bringing Forth New Life

The LORD dealt with Sarah as he had said, and the LORD did for Sarah as he had promised.

(Genesis 21:1)

Sarah came to know the faithfulness of God through the birth of her son. Despite her old age, God broke through and fulfilled the promise that Sarah would give birth to a son who would give rise to a great nation. Sarah named him Isaac, meaning "he laughed." Sarah's laughter of disbelief was now turned into laughter of delight at the birth of her son. God brought great joy into Sarah's life through the blessing of the birth of her son.

Our heart naturally takes delight when God uses our lives to bring about goodness in the world. Whenever you say a kind word to another person, help a stranger, or make a choice not to give in to temptation, you should smile with joy too.

What experience in your life has caused you to laugh with delight?

God, thank you for always keeping your promises. Help me take delight in their fulfillment in my life.

• To go deeper: Read Genesis 21:1–8.

Sarah: Graced with Faith

Sarah died at Kiriath-arba (that is, Hebron) in the land of Canaan; and Abraham went in to mourn for Sarah and to weep for her.

(Genesis 23:2)

At the close of Sarah's life, her family must have recounted her witness of faith in God. Through the legacy of Sarah's son, Isaac, God is known by many people throughout the world. God found Sarah a willing servant involved in bringing faith to life in others. Sarah was graced because ultimately she and Abraham trusted in God. She was buried in a simple tomb in the cave of Machpelah, which many visit today in the city of Hebron. Sarah, the mother of faith, continues to lead others on their journey of faith today.

Who has been a person of faith, like Sarah, in your life? How has that person been a willing witness and servant of God?

Mother Sarah, thank you for your dedication to God and your family. You continue to grace us with your faith.

- To go deeper: Read Genesis 23:1–20.

Hagar: Slave Girl of Sarah

> And [the angel of the Lord] said, "Hagar, slave-girl of [Sarah], where have you come from and where are you going?"
>
> (Genesis 16:8)

In ancient cultures, slavery and polygamy were acceptable practices. Hagar was one of the slaves of Abraham's wife, Sarah. Sarah, who was barren, gave permission for her slave to marry Abraham in order to bear a son. Hagar's story of mistreatment and rescue teach us that although slaves may not have had legal rights in biblical times, God still considered them precious and protected; God guided and loved them.

God loves all people no matter their status, gender, color, or culture. All men, women, and children are created by God and are called to participate in God's plan of salvation. We are called to love all people and work to free ourselves and others from physical and spiritual slavery.

What are some of the things people become enslaved to today?

God of love and justice, free us from those things that lead us away from you.

- To go deeper: Read Galatians 4:21—5:1.

Hagar: Pride and Jealousy

> When [Hagar] saw that she had conceived, she looked with contempt on her mistress. . . . Then [Sarah] dealt harshly with [Hagar] and she ran away.
>
> (Genesis 16:4,6)

Hagar was sent by her mistress, Sarah, to produce an heir for Abraham. When Hagar became pregnant, she treated Sarah with contempt, and Sarah in turn was mean to her pregnant servant girl. Hagar's situation became so unbearable that she ran away into the wilderness.

Pride and jealousy often set in motion a downward spiral of violence. Some are angry because they can't have what they want, and others flaunt their good fortune, fueling the fires of jealousy even further. When you flaunt your looks, your athletic successes, your good grades, or your family's wealth, trouble cannot be long in coming.

Have you ever been jealous of others? How do you react when others are jealous of you?

God of the fortunate and unfortunate, heal me of all jealousy and pride.

- To go deeper: Read Genesis 16:1–6.

Hagar: Encountering God

> So [Hagar] named the LORD who spoke to her, "You are El-roi"; for she said, "Have I really seen God and remained alive after seeing him?"
>
> (Genesis 16:13)

Having found Hagar beside a stream of water, God's messenger asked Hagar what brought her to the wilderness. Hagar told the angel she was running away from her mistress, who had mistreated her. The angel responded by telling Hagar to return to her mistress. He said God had taken notice of Hagar's suffering. Hagar's response to the messenger is one of awe that she, a woman and a slave, had encountered the God of Israel and lived.

When we feel hurt or rejected by our family, it is natural to also feel abandoned by God. Hagar's story reminds us that God never abandons us. Many people tell of times when someone gave them a word of hope or kindness when they most needed to hear it.

When have you unexpectedly encountered a "messenger" of God?

Lord, hear the cry of the poor, especially those who have no one to turn to.

- To go deeper: Read Genesis 16:7–15.

Hagar: Trusting in God

> Hagar bore Abram a son; and Abram named his son . . . Ishmael.
>
> (Genesis 16:15)

Despite the possibility of being mistreated by Sarah again, Hagar went back to the camp of Abraham as the angel had instructed her. There she had a son, which fulfilled the promise God had made to Hagar. Abraham named the boy Ishmael and rejoiced at the birth of his son.

Even though Hagar was not one of Abraham's tribe, she trusted in God's messenger. Her faithfulness did not go unnoticed, and God fulfilled the promise he made to her. God does not want us to be in abusive situations. When we find ourselves in those situations, we need to trust that God is with us and not lose hope. We need to ask God for strength and guidance, and look for the help that is there for us.

When have you done something as an act of faith?

Lord, help me not to fear following your word. Rescue me when I am a victim of injustice.

• To go deeper: Read Genesis 17:20–27.

Hagar: Hopeless Again

> [Hagar] said, "Do not let me look on the death of the child."
>
> (Genesis 21:16)

A son, her only child, was all Hagar had. After being cast out by Abraham into the desert with her son (Abraham had God's assurance that Hagar and Ishmael would be okay), Hagar collapsed in tears when the little bread and water she had was gone. Desperate, she laid the child in the shade under a bush and walked some distance from him so as not to hear his cries, and she prepared to die.

Hagar might have had more hope if she had focused on God's earlier assistance when she fled into the dessert. How easy it is to forget the times when God provided the help we desperately needed! Wouldn't our lives be easier if we remembered those times and trusted in God?

Single women and children suffer the most from poverty and hunger. What can you do to support a local effort to feed and protect women and children?

Make a list of times when you worried about something, but things worked out okay in the end. Thank God for helping you through those times of worry and desperation.

- To go deeper: Read Genesis 21:8–10,14–16.

Hagar: God Helps Us Help Ourselves

> God called to Hagar from heaven, and said to her, "What troubles you, Hagar? Do not be afraid; for God has heard the voice of the boy."
>
> (Genesis 21:17)

A tender detail in the harsh story of the slave woman, we are told that God took notice of Hagar's and Ishmael's suffering and sent an angel to comfort them. God then opened Hagar's eyes so she was able to see a well of fresh, cool water nearby.

The story of Hagar is really about God's seeing the plight of the oppressed and answering their cries for help. God does not magically fix Hagar's situation, but opens her eyes so she can discover the solution to her problem. God cares for us and wants to help us, but we also must make good choices for ourselves.

When have you asked God to help you and then discovered a solution to your problem?

God, don't let fear blind me to the solutions to my problems. Help me to know what actions I can take to help myself.

• To go deeper: Read Genesis 21:15–19.

Hagar: Promises Kept

"Come lift up the boy and hold him fast with your hand, for I will make a great nation of him."

(Genesis 21:18)

Hagar, now a single mother, was left to raise her son on her own. Without the security of community and wealth that Abraham's protection provided, Hagar and Ishmael's future was grim. God's messenger encouraged Hagar and told her to lift up her son and support him, because God had plans for Ishmael. God kept his promise, and Ishmael grew into a strong man. He eventually took an Egyptian wife and is believed to be the patriarch of the Arab peoples and the Muslim faith.

Hagar and Ishmael could see only their present situation and had to trust that God's promise would eventually come true. The fulfillment of God's promise did not take place until long after their death.

What promises have been made to you that require a great deal of trust on your part?

God, help me trust that your promises to me will be fulfilled, even if they are not realized in my lifetime.

- To go deeper: Read Genesis 21:20–21, Psalm 112.

Isaac: Finding a Lifetime Friend

"O LORD, the God of my master Abraham . . . let the young woman who comes out to draw, to whom I shall say, 'Please give me a little water from your jar to drink,' and who will say to me, 'Drink, and I will draw for your camels also'—let her be the woman whom the LORD has appointed for my master's son."

(Genesis 24:42–44)

Finding the right wife for his son Isaac was a major concern for Abraham. Abraham's servant took very seriously the task given him by his master and offered a prayer, asking for a sign so he would select the right woman. This sign would assure the servant of finding a God-fearing spouse for Isaac. As you develop friendships, it is wise to ask God's help in choosing good, kind, and faithful friends—those who will be friends for life.

Have you asked God to help you find faithful friends as companions on your life's journey?

Ever-living Lord, faithful friend of all who call on you, fill my life with friends who will help me stay close to you.

• To go deeper: Read Genesis 24:1–48.

Isaac: Rebekah, the Love of His Life

> Then Isaac brought her into his mother Sarah's tent.
> He took Rebekah, and she became his wife; and
> he loved her. So Isaac was comforted after his
> mother's death.
>
> (Genesis 24:67)

The death of a loved one, especially a parent, can be devastating. Isaac knew that pain in the loss of his mother, Sarah. Having Rebekah come into his life at this time of sorrow was a gift from God. Isaac could share the love in his heart with his wife.

Often in times of grief and loss, we seek to find someone to love us. Isaac is a marvelous model of how reaching out and sharing our love with others, even when we are in pain, can be a source of comfort and healing.

When has grief become an opportunity for you to reach out to others?

God of all consolation, help me, especially in times of sorrow and loss, to share the love in my heart with others.

- To go deeper: Read Genesis 24:50–67.

Isaac: Sibling Rivalry

The LORD granted [Isaac's] prayer, and his wife Rebekah conceived. The children struggled together within her.

(Genesis 25:21–22)

Our ancestry in Christ is filled with sibling rivalry, conflict, and struggles. Isaac's twin sons began their battles before they were even born—when they were "womb-mates." Struggles, disagreements, and jealousies are often a part of family life, especially between siblings. This can be very painful and make you wonder, where is God in all this? But as the story of Isaac's sons unfolds, we see God's grace at work even amid tumultuous relationships.

How would you describe your relationship with other family members? How is God working amid these relationships?

Jesus, my brother, guide me in my treatment of other family members. May jealousies and struggles never stand in the way of your desire to unite us.

• To go deeper: Read Genesis 25:19–26.

Isaac: The Favored Son

Isaac loved Esau, because he was fond of game.

(Genesis 25:28)

It is not unusual for one child in a family to feel that his or her parent favors one sibling over another. In Isaac's family, this favoritism was evident. Isaac favored Esau over his brother Jacob because Esau was a skillful hunter and brought meat home to eat. Jacob responded by using his cooking skills and trickery to win his brother's birthright and ultimately his father's favor and blessing.

Feeling as though we do not measure up to our parents' ideal can be devastating. However, instead of resorting to trickery or trying to manipulate our parents by going out of our way to please them, we are called to trust that God will guide us through those feelings.

What are your experiences of being favored by a parent, or of not measuring up to a parent's ideal?

God of all acceptance and love, guide me to realize that you are not partial, but loving and accepting of all.

• To go deeper: Read Genesis 25:24–34.

Isaac: A Change of Plans

> The LORD appeared to Isaac and said, "Do not go down to Egypt; settle in the land that I shall show you. Reside in this land as an alien, and I will be with you, and will bless you."
>
> (Genesis 26:2–3)

When faced with difficulties, Isaac devised a plan that he thought best for him—he would avoid the famine of the area and go to Egypt. God, however, had other plans. God's plan meant that Isaac would have to live as an alien in a foreign and unfamiliar land. God's promise to be with Isaac and to bless him was the support Isaac needed to make the shift from what he wanted to what God asked of him.

The plans we make often do not turn out as we expect. Being open and flexible, as Isaac was, can bring a blessing and an awareness of God's presence.

Amid changing plans, how open are you to God's will?

Abiding God, teach me to stay open to your call and to find you amid the unexpected.

• To go deeper: Read Genesis 26:1–5.

Isaac: Envy's Object

> Isaac had possessions of flocks and herds, and a great household, so that the Philistines envied him.
>
> (Genesis 26:14)

Responding with resentment and envy to those who possess more than we do is not an unusual experience. Most of us are keenly aware of those who have the latest gadgets and the most possessions. Like the Philistines, it is easy for us to envy those who have more than we do. Isaac was envied for his flocks, herds, and great household. Nothing is said about him flaunting his wealth. He simply had a lot of possessions.

There will always be people in our lives who have more than we do. Our attitude toward them says more about us than it does about them. Being consumed by envy toward others can keep us from enjoying their presence and appreciating them for who they are as human beings.

What is your attitude toward those who have more than you do?

Keep me, Lord, from letting feelings of envy prevent me from accepting those who have more than I do.

• To go deeper: Read Genesis 26:1–33.

Isaac: Tricked by the Trickster

> [Isaac] said, "Are you really my son Esau?" [Jacob] answered, "I am." Then [Isaac] said, "Bring it [the food] to me, that I may eat of my son's game and bless you."
>
> (Genesis 27:24–25)

Realizing that someone else is receiving the recognition, honor, or blessing that you rightly deserve is a pain unlike all others. The cry, "It isn't fair," rises from the depths of one's soul. Being old and blind, Isaac didn't realize his son Jacob (whose name means "the trickster") was pretending to be his older, favored brother Esau. Esau, as the oldest, had a blessing coming. Through deception, Jacob took the blessing from Esau. Once Isaac pronounced the blessing, it couldn't be taken back, even if Jacob had gotten it dishonestly.

How do you handle situations where others get credit for what you have done?

God of all justice, be with me in times when life seems unfair and others receive what I deserve. Bless me with a gentle spirit.

- To go deeper: Read Genesis 27:1–46.

Rebekah: Destined to Be Chosen

Abraham said to his servant, . . . "Go to my country and my kindred and get a wife for my son Isaac."

(Genesis 24:2,4)

Rebekah, descendant of Abraham's brother Nahor, was unaware of the events that would change her life when she went to the spring that day. Under the blazing summer sun, this veiled, dark-haired, olive-skinned woman sweated as she fetched huge jars of water from the well for her family's needs. When a stranger asked her for a drink, she not only cheerfully gave him water but proceeded to draw water for his camels! This was the right one, the servant thought—hardworking, generous, and of a believing family. Rebekah would become Isaac's wife and become a link in the family tree of the Messiah.

The Scriptures record how God actively chose the people who would pass on the faith from generation to generation. Who are the keepers of the faith in your family?

God of all, help me to appreciate the faith that has been handed on to me and to do my part to share my faith with future generations.

• To go deeper: Read Genesis 24:1–27.

Rebekah: Answering God's Call

And [Rebekah's brother and mother] called Rebekah, and said to her, "Will you go with this man?"

(Genesis 24:58)

In choosing a wife for Isaac, Abraham's servant watched closely for just the right woman. Every young woman was eager to be pleasing to the men of eligible families. Rebekah, though unassuming and hard at work with her chores, was gracious and helpful. Her family loved her very much and were not eager for her to leave home.

The Book of Genesis notes something special in this arranged marriage. Rebekah's family asked her if she wanted to marry Isaac and go to his home, which was a great distance away. In this culture, women were often not even consulted about whom they wanted to marry! Rebekah seemed to know she was part of a greater plan.

How willing are you to say yes to what God is asking of you?

God of all plans and outcomes, may I be generous and kind to others and open to the plans you have for me.

- To go deeper: Read Genesis 24:28–60.

Rebekah: Love at First Sight

Rebekah looked up, and when she saw Isaac, she slipped quickly from the camel. . . . [Isaac] took Rebekah, and she became his wife; and he loved her.

(Genesis 24:64,67)

After the servant selected Rebekah as Isaac's wife, arrangements were made to take her to Isaac's family. Rebekah left with her family's blessing and traveled by caravan to her new home. As they neared their destination, Rebekah must have wondered: Will he think I am attractive? Will he love me as my family and friends have loved me?

When the caravan arrived, Rebekah saw a man walking alone in the fields. Learning that the lone man was her future husband, Isaac, she quickly slipped from the camel's back and covered herself with a veil. Isaac embraced Rebekah—it was love at first sight!

Do you think love at first sight is possible? What does love mean to you?

God of goodness and love, on this day when we celebrate love, I pray for my parents and all married couples. May their love be strong and faithful.

- To go deeper: Read Genesis 24:59–67.

Rebekah: Barren!

> "Isaac prayed to the LORD for his wife, because she was barren; and the LORD granted his prayer."
>
> (Genesis 25:21)

The greatest disgrace for a woman in ancient times was to be barren, or unable to bear children. A husband was dependant on a strong and healthy wife to give him many offspring to ensure survival of the tribe. Rebekah suffered the disgrace of barrenness for many years. As Isaac and Rebekah waited for a family, their love grew strong and helped them to withstand the shame of Rebekah's being barren. Then, in answer to Isaac's prayers, Rebekah conceived. Their time of waiting and suffering had come to an end! Isaac and Rebekah must have rejoiced, knowing that the line of Abraham's family would continue.

Have you ever prayed for something that you really wanted for a long time? Was your prayer answered the way you expected?

Gracious God, help me be persistent and patient in presenting my prayers to you.

• To go deeper: Read Genesis 25:7–21.

Rebekah: Double Trouble

> When [Rebekah's] time to give birth was at hand, there were twins in her womb.
>
> (Genesis 25:24)

Rebekah's pregnancy was a difficult one. Early on she felt that she carried not one, but two children. They were lively, and she felt them wrestle within her womb. The months of waiting were full of delight and worry as Rebekah wondered: Will my children be healthy? How do I keep them safe and well? Finally the day arrived, and the twins were born, already struggling and fighting. To this day, the descendants of Esau and Jacob do not get along.

Parents want their children to get along and love each other. It must have caused Rebekah great pain to see her two sons always competing with each other. Someday you may experience this firsthand if you have children

How do you get along with siblings or other family members? Are you a peacemaker or a source of conflict?

Father, Son, and Holy Spirit, I want us to be a happy family. Help me do my part to make it happen.

• To go deeper: Read Genesis 25:21–26.

Rebekah: Mom's Favorite

. . . but Rebekah loved Jacob.

(Genesis 25:28)

It is hard to believe that a mother would have a favorite child, but Rebekah did, and it changed the course of biblical history. Of her twin sons, Rebekah favored Jacob, perhaps because Jacob was gentler and enjoyed being around the tents with the women rather than in the fields with the men. In any case, Rebekah was determined that her husband's blessing and inheritance be given to Jacob rather than Esau. Rebekah devised a plan that helped Jacob trick her husband into blessing Jacob rather than Esau.

This story is not really about Rebekah's deceit but about God's defying human expectations. Often in the Bible, God chooses the people who are considered weak and unimportant to carry out God's plan.

When has someone you thought was an unlikely choice been given a prestigious honor or task?

God, help me see your presence in the lives of those I consider to be weak or unworthy.

• To go deeper: Read Genesis 27:1–29.

Rebekah: A Mother's Wish

> "If Jacob marries one of the Hittite women such as these, one of the women of the land, what good will my life be to me?"
>
> (Genesis 27:46)

As youth grow to maturity, parents constantly worry about who and what are influencing their son or daughter. Rebekah was concerned about Jacob and his friends, especially whom he might marry. She did not want him to marry a woman from the tribes who worshiped false gods and did not follow the commands of God.

Sometimes youth "worship" the false gods of our culture: designer clothes, drugs, alcohol, fast cars, gadgets, and other material things. When these things become the main focus of our lives, we can be lured away from what is really important—healthy relationships with family, friends, and the God who created and cares for us.

What are the things that lure you away from God and from healthy relationships with your family or friends?

God, keep me from being caught up in things that lure me away from you and healthy relationships with my family and friends.

• To go deeper: Read Genesis 27:46—28:1.

Jacob: Third Patriarch

> His brother came out, with his hand gripping Esau's heel; so he was named Jacob.
>
> (Genesis 25:26)

Even though Jacob was a twin, he was the second-born son. Both the birthright and Isaac's blessing, according to cultural tradition, should have gone to Esau, the firstborn. But through God's design, Jacob gained both and became the father of twelve sons, whose descendants became the twelve tribes of Israel. The promise Abraham and Sarah received from God—that their descendants would be as numerous as the stars—was fulfilled in Jacob and his sons.

God uses the circumstances of our lives to make known the divine plan for each of us. As with Jacob, our understanding of God's plan for us takes time to unfold.

What do you see as God's plan for your life, even if it may be only partial at this time?

God, let me see your hand active in each stage of my life.

• To go deeper: Read Genesis 25:19–34.

Jacob: The Ladder to Heaven

> I am the LORD, the God of Abraham your father and the God of Isaac.
>
> (Genesis 28:13)

One night, while traveling to the house of his uncle Laban, Jacob had a dream. In his dream, Jacob saw a stairway leading from the ground into heaven, and on the stairway were messengers going up and coming down. In the dream, God appeared and affirmed that Jacob was to follow in the footsteps of his father, Isaac, and his grandfather, Abraham. Jacob was told that he was the favored son in whom God's promise of a mighty nation would be fulfilled. Jacob named the site of his dream Bethel, "House of God," and honored it as a sacred place.

There are sacred places in our own lives where we feel God is truly present. It is as if the location has a direct connection to heaven. What place has been a sacred space for you?

Do you invite God to journey with you daily, or do you confine God to your sacred space?

God, you break through into our world in many different ways. Help me recognize your presence.

- To go deeper: Read Genesis 28:10–22.

Jacob: An Uncle's Welcome

> When Laban heard the news about his sister's son Jacob, he ran to meet him; he embraced him and kissed him.
>
> (Genesis 29:13)

After Jacob revealed his identity to Rachel—that her father, Laban, was his uncle—Rachel went to tell her father and her whole family. As soon as he heard the news, Laban ran to greet Jacob and welcomed him with an embrace and then invited him into his house. After Jacob told Laban who he was, Laban responded, "Surely you are my bone and my flesh!" (Genesis 29:14).

We are blessed in a significant way when we are able to reveal our true identity with our family members. We are doubly blessed when they embrace us for who we are and claim in a profound way that we are a part of them.

How easy or difficult is it for you to be open with your family and reveal your true identity?

God, give me the confidence I need to always be myself so my family can embrace the true me.

- To go deeper: Read Genesis 29:1–14.

Jacob: Tricked by Laban

> Jacob loved Rachel; so he said, "I will serve you seven years for your younger daughter Rachel."
>
> (Genesis 29:18)

Arranged marriages were usually negotiated by the parents, but in Jacob's case, Jacob had already expressed his love for Rachel and made the arrangement to pay the *mohar,* the gift given by the groom to the father of the bride. But the story takes an interesting twist when Jacob, the trickster, is tricked by Laban. After working seven years to win Rachel as his wife, Jacob is instead given Leah, the older daughter. When Jacob discovers he has been deceived, he agrees to work seven more years in order to marry Rachel, as men were allowed to have more than one wife at that time.

Sometimes what we do to others is returned to us. The same trickery that Jacob used against his brother, Esau, is now used by Laban against Jacob.

How has your own dishonesty or trickery been like a boomerang and returned to you?

God, help me to deal honestly with others and to rely on truth rather than trickery.

- To go deeper: Read Genesis 29:15–30.

Jacob: Wrestling with God

> Jacob was left alone; and a man wrestled with him until daybreak.
>
> (Genesis 32:24)

Before reuniting with his brother Esau, Jacob spent the night alone near the River Jabbok. It was there that Jacob wrestled with a stranger until dawn. Jacob prevailed even after the stranger struck Jacob's hip socket and bruised it, making him limp. At dawn, the stranger not only blessed Jacob but also told him, "You shall no longer be called Jacob, but Israel, for you have striven with God and with humans" (Genesis 32:28). The name Israel means "he who struggles with God."

Sometimes our own restless nights are the result of struggles in our lives. We may perhaps be "wrestling with God" like Jacob. These struggles can lead us to be changed people, more aware of God's direction in our lives.

When have you wrestled with God? How have you been changed by the experience?

God, bless me in my struggles and let me always be changed for the better.

- To go deeper: Read Genesis 32:23–33.

Jacob: An Unexpected Embrace

But Esau ran to meet him, and embraced him.

(Genesis 33:4)

After twenty years apart, Jacob readied himself for a reunion with his brother Esau. Because Esau was angry with Jacob when he left, Jacob was expecting the worst. When the moment arrived, and Jacob and Esau saw each other, the reunion exceeded Jacob's expectations. Esau ran to meet Jacob and fully embraced him. The two brothers were finally reconciled. Jacob and Esau were once again able to build upon their relationship with each other.

Life is filled with reunions of many different kinds. Reunions between individuals where there is unresolved tension can be very difficult. However, if we are aware of our own shortcomings and choose to reconcile with someone because the relationship is important, the reunion may exceed our expectations.

Which reunions in your life have exceeded your expectations? Why?

God, help me reconcile the relationships in my life that are in need of healing.

• To go deeper: Read Genesis 33:1–17.

Jacob: Grieving a Deep Loss

> Then Jacob tore his garments, and put sackcloth on his loins, and mourned for his son many days.
>
> (Genesis 37:34)

When Jacob sent his young son Joseph to deliver a message to his brothers, there was no way Jacob could have known he was sending Joseph into harm's way. After selling Joseph into slavery, Joseph's brothers concealed what they did by making it appear as if a wild beast had attacked and devoured Joseph. Jacob mourned his son's apparent death for many days. No one, not even his other sons, were able to console him.

Dealing with the death of a person we have loved deeply is hard. We mourn for that person because he or she was a key relationship in our lives. At first nothing consoles us, but eventually, we may find consolation in knowing that in life after death, we will once again be reunited with our loved one.

Whose death has left a hole in your heart?

God, touch my sadness with understanding and peace.

• To go deeper: Read Genesis 37:12–35.

Joseph: The Boastful Dreamer

> But when [Joseph] told [the dream] to his father and
> to his brothers, his father rebuked him, and said to
> him, "What kind of dream is this that you have had?
> Shall we indeed come, I and your mother and your
> brothers, and bow to the ground before you?"
>
> (Genesis 37:10–11)

As the first child of Jacob and Rachel, Joseph was the
favored son who had been given a coat of many colors.
Understandably, Joseph's half brothers were jealous. Joseph didn't help the situation when he insisted on sharing
the dreams that pointed to the position of power he would
wield over his family someday.

Prideful arrogance and jealousy are temptations we
all face, especially when we are feeling insecure about
ourselves. The story of Joseph and his brothers provides
an important lesson on how our attitudes and actions can
alienate those closest to us.

When has your attitude or actions alienated friends or
family members?

*Forgive me, Lord, for the times when I have let pride
or jealousy harm my relationships.*

• To go deeper: Read Genesis 37:1–20.

Reuben: A Caring Big Brother

> "Come now, let us kill [Joseph] and throw him into one of the pits." . . . But when Reuben heard it, he delivered him out of their hands, saying, "Let us not take his life."
>
> (Genesis 37:20–21)

Jacob and Leah's firstborn, Reuben, was the typical eldest child. His keen sense of responsibility and desire to care for his siblings saved not only the life of his brother Joseph, but in the end saved the lives of all his brothers, because they would one day need Joseph to save their family. Reuben showed courage in trying to make the right choice even when his brothers were choosing an evil action.

Peer pressure has the power to influence us to make choices for good or ill. To stand against peer pressure when we are being urged to do what we know is wrong takes a great commitment to goodness, the kind of goodness Reuben demonstrated.

In what ways has peer pressure influenced your decisions?

Like Reuben, Lord, may I always have the courage to make good choices.

• To go deeper: Read Genesis 37:21–36.

Judah: The Bright-Idea Brother

> Then Judah said to his brothers, "What profit is it if we kill our brother and conceal his blood? Come, let us sell him to the Ishmaelites."
>
> (Genesis 37:26–27)

Judah was another, older half brother of Joseph who told his siblings it was wrong to kill Joseph because it would not profit anyone. Judah suggested that Joseph be sold instead of being killed. Although Judah did not go along with his other brothers in wanting to kill Joseph, he still did not choose rightly or well. The bottom line for Judah, as it is for many people today, was profit.

Taking time to reflect on decisions that will affect one's life and the lives of others is a sign of growing into adulthood. It is important that we determine if we are doing the right thing or are simply concerned with how it benefits us.

When have you been grateful that reflection on a decision allowed you to do the right thing instead of acting only for your own gain?

Counselor God, help me to reflect on the decisions I make and to choose wisely and well.

- To go deeper: Read Genesis 37:25–36.

Benjamin: Joseph's Baby Brother

> Then [Joseph] looked up and saw his brother Benjamin, his mother's son, and said, "Is this your youngest brother, of whom you spoke to me? God be gracious to you, my son!"
>
> (Genesis 43:29)

Benjamin was Jacob's youngest son whose mother, Rachel, died in giving birth to him. Benjamin and Joseph were the only two sons Jacob had with his beloved wife Rachel. The bond between the three men was strong and deep. Even though Benjamin didn't recognize Joseph, he heard his brother's words of tender concern and blessing.

Young people tend to focus on moving beyond family; however, the bond with siblings and other family members continues to be important. Kind words and caring ways are vital to establishing ties that will endure both good times and bad times.

How would you describe your relationship with members of your family?

God of all families, give me the grace to be kind in words and actions toward my family.

- To go deeper: Read Genesis 43:26–34.

Joseph and Benjamin: Big Boys Do Cry!

"You must tell my father how greatly I am honored in Egypt, and all that you have seen. Hurry and bring my father down here." Then [Joseph] fell upon his brother Benjamin's neck and wept, while Benjamin wept upon his neck.

(Genesis 45:13–14)

Benjamin, like his brother Joseph, was overcome with emotion as he realized the reunion and reconnection he and his brothers were experiencing. Benjamin's one and only full-blooded brother—whom he thought was dead— was standing before him! Though an ancient adage proclaims, "Big boys don't cry," Benjamin and Joseph freely expressed the depth of emotion they were feeling as they held each other and wept. Feeling and expressing deep emotions is a precious experience of being human. Christ himself shed tears of deep emotion.

When have you felt something deeply and expressed those feelings in tears of joy or pain?

Tender God, teach me to enter into the joys and sorrows of life unashamed of expressing my feelings in tears of gladness or sadness.

• To go deeper: Read Genesis 45:4–15.

Joseph: Revealing the Truth

> Then Joseph could no longer control himself before
> all those who stood by him. . . . Joseph said to
> his brothers, "I am Joseph. Is my father still alive?"
> But his brothers could not answer him, so dismayed
> were they at his presence.
>
> (Genesis 45:1,3)

Someone once said, "The truth will make you free, but
first it will make you miserable." This seems to be Joseph's
experience. He recognizes the men standing before him
as the brothers who sold him to traders after having had
second thoughts about killing him. Joseph can barely
control himself, and in the midst of loud weeping, he
tells his brothers the truth of who he is. Joseph's revelation
leaves his brothers terrified and speechless.

The power of truth can never be overestimated. Joseph's
willingness to face the truth is the start to the healing his
family needs.

When has speaking the truth or hearing it spoken
brought you healing?

*God of all truth, grant me the insight, wisdom, and
courage to speak the truth and to hear it with an open
heart.*

- To go deeper: Read Genesis 45:1–15.

Joseph: Forgiving Family

> Then Joseph said to his brothers, ". . . I am your brother, Joseph, whom you sold into Egypt. And now do not be distressed, or angry with yourselves, because you sold me here; for God sent me before you to preserve life."
>
> (Genesis 45:4–5)

With these few words, Joseph offered his brothers forgiveness and the hope of healing. As the lord of Pharaoh's house, Joseph could have punished his brothers or gotten even with them for selling him into slavery. Joseph, however, chose to forgive because he recognized that God was using the situation to save everyone's life.

The pain of being hurt by family or friends touches the very core of our being. Joseph models for us the way to forgiveness and how to see God's causing good to come from even sinful choices.

When have you experienced being forgiven for the wrongs you have done?

Compassionate God, help me forgive others as you have forgiven me. May I experience your presence in the difficult situations of my life.

• To go deeper: Read Genesis 45:16–28.

Joseph: Gone Is the Grudge

Realizing their father was dead, Joseph's brothers said, "What if Joseph still bears a grudge against us and pays us back in full for all the wrong that we did to him? . . . But Joseph said to them, "Do not be afraid! Am I in the place of God?"

(Genesis 50:15,19)

Joseph not only willingly forgave his brothers but also assured them that they would have nothing to fear in the future. Joseph realized he was not God, and therefore he did not judge or punish his brothers for the pain they caused him. He did not bear a grudge.

In a world where most people find ways to get even, retaliate, or seek revenge, Joseph simply let God be God. Joseph, like Christ, is a model example of how to forgive with no strings attached.

What do you need to do to let go of the grudges in your life?

Gentle God of compassion and forgiveness, give me what I need to forgive others. May the desire to return evil for evil never dominate my life.

• To go deeper: Read Genesis 50:15–24.

Moses: The Law Giver

She named him Moses, "because," she said, "I drew him out of the water."

(Exodus 2:10)

Moses is one of the most important persons in the Old Testament. He is honored as the one who gave God's people the Law, which has guided them to the present day. Moses was a shy person. However, Yahweh determined that Moses was the one to save the Israelites from the harsh slavery of Egypt. This reluctant hero was courageous before the power of Pharaoh and tenacious as he led the Israelites from slavery into a moral life shaped by the Ten Commandments.

Like Moses, we often are too quick to focus on our own flaws and inadequacies. We dismiss the possibility that God could be calling us to do great things. In spite of our human weakness, God is able to use us to free others from the things that deny them their human dignity.

What flaws or inadequacies keep you from answering God's call to help others?

God of Moses, help me overcome my human weaknesses in order to lead others to you.

• To go deeper: Read Exodus 2:1–10.

Moses: Born into Danger

> Then Pharaoh commanded all his people, "Every boy that is born to the Hebrews you shall throw into the Nile."
>
> (Exodus 1:22)

Moses was born into a world of danger. His life was threatened from the moment he was born. Through the cleverness of his mother, Jochebed, and under the watchful eye of his sister, Miriam, Moses was adopted by Pharaoh's daughter. God provided Moses safety in the house of the same Pharaoh who sent forth the decree ordering all Hebrew male children drowned in the Nile River. God had favored Moses from birth, but God also had great expectations of him.

Most of us do not live in an environment where our lives are threatened from birth. But, like God did with Moses, God has favored us with many gifts and blessings and expects us to use those gifts to bring about a just world.

What gifts and blessings has God given you? In what ways is God challenging you to use them?

God, protector and provider of all, thank you for the generosity you have shown me.

- To go deeper: Read Exodus 1:1–22.

Moses: God Speaks

> Then [God] said, "Come no closer! Remove the sandals from your feet, for the place on which you are standing is holy ground."
>
> (Exodus 3:5)

Moses was attracted to the burning bush because he saw that it was not being consumed. As Moses drew closer, God told Moses to take off his shoes in reverence of the holy ground he was standing on. The same God who called Abraham, Isaac, and Jacob now called Moses to the noble task of leading God's Chosen People out of slavery in Egypt and back to the Promised Land. Moses doubted his ability to stand against mighty Pharaoh, but God assured Moses he did not go alone, God would always be with him.

God speaks to each of us and challenges us to help free others from the various forms of slavery—addiction, abuse, and so on—prevalent today.

How does God get your attention? Once God has your attention, are you open to hearing what God has to say?

God who calls us closer, help me to be open to hearing your voice.

• To go deeper: Read Exodus 3:1–15.

Moses: Pleading for His People

> Moses and Aaron went to Pharaoh and said, "Thus says the LORD, the God of Israel, 'Let my people go.'"
>
> (Exodus 5:1)

Despite Pharaoh's defiance and refusal to allow God's people to go free, Moses was a persistent spokesperson for God. Time and time again, Moses went before Pharaoh as God's advocate and requested that the Israelites be freed from slavery. Because of Moses's faithfulness to God, the freedom of God's people was eventually won.

Advocates who call for justice are needed in our world today. Because of the persistence of specific individuals, freedom from oppression is won for many. Some examples of modern-day advocates are Mother Teresa of Calcutta, Nelson Mandela, and Dr. Martin Luther King Jr.

How can you be an advocate for justice?

God, let me be an advocate for those who suffer injustice today. Help me be persistent in seeking justice for all.

- To go deeper: Read Exodus 5:1–13.

Moses: Reliant on God

> Strike the rock, and water will come out of it, so that the people may drink.
>
> (Exodus 17:6)

Moses was an instrument of God's grace in the life of the Israelites as they made their way through the desert. Interceding on behalf of the Israelites, Moses petitioned Yahweh for fresh water when there was none or when it was bitter tasting. When the people cried for food, Moses promised that God would send manna and quail. Despite the constant complaints of the people and their impatience with God, Moses continued to rely on God completely. Moses's example eventually helped the Israelites to also rely on God.

Our complete reliance on God can help others understand that God does provide for all our needs. But we may have to listen to the grumbling of some people who are not satisfied with God's timing.

When have you had to rely completely on God? How was your reliance a witness to others?

God of providence, we rely on you because we know you will not disappoint us.

- To go deeper: Read Exodus 16:4–15, 17:1–7.

Moses: Lawgiver

Then God delivered all these commandments.

(Exodus 20:1, NAB)

Moses is known as the lawgiver because the Ten Commandments came to the Israelites from God through Moses. Moses helped the Jewish people understand how keeping God's Commandments would unite them as a people and foster human dignity. He showed them how to integrate these standards of morality into their daily life. The Commandments reminded them that they were to live holy lives and to avoid partaking in the immorality and idolatry of their neighbors.

The Ten Commandments continue to function as the moral foundation of Christian life today. Refresh your understanding of the Ten Commandments and their application to your life as a young adult.

How do the Ten Commandments serve as a guide for you in making good moral decisions in your daily life?

God of wisdom and compassion, thank you for giving us the Ten Commandments as a guide for living your law of love.

• To go deeper: Read Exodus 20:1–21.

Moses: Denied the Promised Land

> Then Moses, the servant of the LORD, died there in the land of Moab, at the LORD's command. He was buried in a valley in the land of Moab.
>
> (Deuteronomy 34:5–6)

After leading the Israelites for forty years, Moses died before he was able to cross the Jordan River into the Promised Land. Moses did, however, see a glimpse of the Promised Land from Mount Pisgah in Moab. Moses had been faithful to God in leading the Israelites out of slavery, but Joshua was the one God had chosen to lead the Israelites into Canaan.

Part of the frustration of working hard for a cause or an organization is that we may not see the long-term result of our efforts. It is helpful to remember that we benefit from the people who worked hard to prepare the way for us, and our hard work will prepare the way for those who come after us.

Which task(s) that you have given a great amount of time and hard work to will need to be finished by someone else?

God, give me the strength to do my very best even with those tasks that are someone else's to finish.

• To go deeper: Read Deuteronomy 34:1–12.

Aaron: The Liberator's Voice

[Aaron] indeed shall speak for [Moses] to the people.

(Exodus 4:16)

Aaron is mentioned often in the Book of Exodus, but seldom does his name appear before that of his brother Moses. Aaron and Moses stood side by side in bargaining with Pharaoh for freedom for the Israelites, who had been cruelly oppressed in Egypt. When God selected Moses as the one to save his people, Moses told God that he was not eloquent enough to speak before Pharaoh. So God told Moses that his brother Aaron would do the talking.

As Christians, God also asks us to speak up when others are being treated unfairly. There may be times when we are afraid to speak on behalf of another. If we rely on God, no matter what the circumstance, we will surely find the strength needed to be an advocate for others.

How might God be calling you to speak on behalf of those experiencing injustice?

God of Moses and Aaron, help me overcome my fears and speak out against injustice.

- To go deeper: Read Exodus 4:10–31.

Aaron: The Go-Between

Each one threw down his staff, and they became snakes; but Aaron's staff swallowed up theirs.

(Exodus 7:12)

To convince Pharaoh to let the Jewish people leave Egypt and carve out their own homeland, God gave Aaron miraculous powers. Under the direction of Moses, Aaron threw down his walking staff in front of Pharaoh, and it turned into a snake. Pharaoh's sorcerers did the same, but their staffs were swallowed up by Aaron's staff.

God worked through Aaron and gave him the power to do wondrous deeds. God also works through us and gives us the ability to demonstrate God's power in the good works we do for others.

When did your good actions bring about a positive change in others? If you could work one miracle, what would it be?

God of wonders, you show us miracles every day. You give courage to the timid, and you quiet the boastful. Give me the power to be a positive influence for change in my world.

• To go deeper: Read Exodus 7:8—8:19.

Aaron: Uphold the Leader

Aaron and Hur held up [Moses's] hands.

(Exodus 17:12)

During a battle with one of Israel's many enemies, Moses took Aaron and another loyal follower, Hur, to the top of a nearby mountain to watch the progress of the battle and to pray for victory. Whenever Moses held up his hands, the Israelites were winning the battle, but when Moses's arm grew tired and he lowered his hands, Israel began to lose. So Aaron and Hur were told to stand on either side of Moses and hold his arms up. This was done until sunset, and Israel won the battle.

Moses, the great leader, needed help. He could not win the battle alone, so he turned to his brother Aaron and a friend for assistance. We also need the support and prayers of others to help us win the battle against sin in our lives.

How has the prayerful support of others helped you through difficult times?

God of Aaron and Hur, may I be a source of support for those who depend on me and always remember to lift up the needs of others in prayer.

• To go deeper: Read Exodus 17:8–13.

Aaron: The Golden Calf

> [Aaron] took the gold from them . . . and cast an
> image of a calf.
>
> (Exodus 32:4)

Aaron's role in the story of the creation of the golden calf
must have been a bitter disappointment for God and for
Moses. Moses had gone up to Mount Sinai to be with
God. Days and weeks went by, and Moses did not return.
A rumor started that he might never return. Without Moses
the people began to doubt God's presence. Instead of
encouraging the people to maintain their faith in the
unseen God, Aaron made a golden idol, worshiping
something they could see.

When we are alone and afraid, when we fail to see
God's presence in our lives, we also may be tempted
to turn to something we can see and touch to give us
comfort. These things, however, only mask our pain and
give us a false sense of hope.

What material things have you turned to in times of
difficulty?

*Ever-present God, give me the grace to turn to you
in times of crisis, and never let me lose sight of you
in my life.*

• To go deeper: Read Exodus 32:1–6.

Aaron: They Made Me Do It!

For Aaron had let them run wild . . .

(Exodus 32:25)

Seeing Israel's wickedness, God sent Moses back to his "perverse people" in a hurry. Moses angrily confronted Aaron and questioned him as to why he had led God's people astray. Aaron used the age-old excuse, "They made me do it!" At a time when the Israelites most needed a leader, Aaron gave in to their demands for a god they could see and touch. Aaron, who had seen the great creative power of God, gave in to the pitiful whining of the crowd.

It is especially difficult to stand up for what we know is right when all our friends are encouraging us to do otherwise. Like the Israelites, we may convince ourselves that God is up on his holy mountain and doesn't care about what we are doing.

When have you given in to peer pressure and done something you know is wrong or offered no resistance when everyone else was doing evil?

Ask God's forgiveness for any times you let others convince you to do something wrong.

• To go deeper: Read Exodus 32:7–34.

Aaron: Consecrated to Holiness

> Then you shall bring Aaron and his sons to the entrance of the tent of meeting, and shall wash them with water, . . . and you shall anoint him and consecrate him, so that he may serve me as priest.
>
> (Exodus 40:12–13)

Aaron and his sons were selected from among the Israelites to lead God's people in prayer and worship. They were washed, anointed, clothed in sacred vestments, and consecrated to the priesthood of God. God selected Aaron and his sons to be models of holiness for God's people.

At Baptism, each of us is cleansed in the baptismal waters, anointed with the oil of chrism, robed in the white garment of holiness, and consecrated as God's priest, prophet, and king. We are called to be models of holiness in our world by living in loving service to God's people.

How are you a model of holiness for others? How is God calling you to serve the Church?

Holy God, give me the wisdom to discern how I am to live out my vocation. Bless the priests, religious, and laypeople who serve my parish so faithfully.

• To go deeper: Read Exodus 29:1–37.

Aaron: Offering Sacrifice

This is the offering that Aaron and his sons shall offer to the Lord. . . .

(Leviticus 6:20)

One of the main tasks of Aaron and his sons as priests was to offer grain and animal sacrifices to God in atonement for people's sins. The Israelites believed some kind of restitution was needed to repair the damage sin had caused not only to the sinner but also to the lives of others touched by the sinner. The priest stood before God in place of the people.

Because Jesus made the ultimate sacrifice on the cross, we no longer need to offer sacrifices for the forgiveness of sins. The sacrifice we are asked to make is to lay down our lives for one another, whether it is patiently living through difficult times or giving up something that is important to us to help someone else.

What sacrifice is God asking you to make?

God, forgive my sins and help me to offer up for the good of others the sufferings and difficulties I experience daily.

• To go deeper: Read Leviticus 6:24—7:7, Psalm 51.

Miriam: Serving from a Distance

> [Moses's] sister stood at a distance, to see what would happen to him.
>
> (Exodus 2:4)

Though we aren't given her name in this biblical passage, Moses's sister, Miriam, is described as watching over her baby brother as he is put in a basket and placed among reeds on the bank of the river. Miriam has the task of staying in the background as she seeks to watch over her brother. Miriam's role isn't glamorous, but it is vital to saving her brother's life.

Part of the idealism of being young is the desire to do great and glorious things. But sometimes what is needed is to remain nameless and at a distance. As Jesus said, "Whoever wishes to become great among you must be your servant" (Mark 10:43).

What experiences have you had of being in the background and remaining nameless as you did the right thing?

God beyond all names, help me to know how to serve behind the scenes, without the need of recognition.

- To go deeper: Read Exodus 2:1–5.

Miriam: From Patience to a Plan

> Then [Moses's] sister said to Pharaoh's daughter, "Shall I go and get you a nurse from the Hebrew women to nurse the child for you?"
>
> (Exodus 2:7)

When the infant Moses was found by Pharaoh's daughter, Miriam sprang to action. She quickly made a plan and fearlessly approached Pharaoh's daughter. Cleverly she arranged for Moses's own mother to nurse Moses!

Heeding God's call to care for others sometimes means waiting and watching, and sometimes it means taking action. Miriam, as she cares for her brother Moses, gives us an example of both experiences. She knows when to wait and when to step forward with a plan. Patience and planning are both essential in our lives as followers of Christ.

How well do you integrate both patience and planning in your life of service to others?

Lord of wondrous patience and planning, help me know when to use both these gifts of service in my life.

• To go deeper: Read Exodus 2:1–7.

Miriam: The Leader of the Band

> Then the prophet Miriam, Aaron's sister, took a tambourine in her hand; and all the women went out after her with tambourines and with dancing.
>
> (Exodus 15:20)

The word *prophet* literally means something like "one who speaks for God." Miriam is the first woman in the Bible to be called a prophet. Contrary to popular belief, a prophet doesn't foretell the future. Recognizing that God's presence was revealed in her people's safe passage through the Red Sea, Miriam told of God's saving power in songs of praise.

Music, especially for teens, can help us express a range of emotions. When we receive good news, or when difficult situations are resolved, we often use music to express the joy we feel.

At times of delight or gratitude, what music best expresses your feelings?

Music-maker God, may your song of praise echo in my heart as I give thanks for all your wonderful works.

- To go deeper: Read Exodus 15:1–21.

Miriam: A Leader of Prayer

And Miriam sang to them: "Sing to the LORD, for he has triumphed gloriously; horse and rider he has thrown into the sea."

(Exodus 15:21)

In Miriam's time, men and women did not dance together. So when the women needed someone to lead them in expressing their gratitude for God's guidance through the Red Sea, Miriam stepped up to the task. She led the women in a song of praise for God's glorious work.

Stepping into a leadership role can be challenging. Thankfully, many young people do see themselves as being leaders, especially leaders of prayer. God calls people of both genders and of all ages to participate in and serve the Church.

In what areas of your life might God be calling you to lead others? How are you being called to lead others in prayer?

Counselor God, give me a discerning heart so I will know how you are calling me to lead others, especially in prayer and service.

• To go deeper: Read Exodus 15:19–21.

Miriam: The Green-Eyed Monster

> While they were at Hazeroth, Miriam and Aaron
> spoke against Moses because of the Cushite woman
> whom he had married . . . ; and they said, "Has
> the LORD spoken only through Moses? Has he not
> spoken through us also?"
>
> (Numbers 12:1–2)

Sometimes when others seem to get all the honors and attention, our ability to see things clearly is affected. We see everything in light of what we are being denied and in what others are doing wrong. We feel envious and maybe even want to attack the people getting the atten-tion. Jealousy brought Miriam and Aaron to attack their brother, Moses, because they too wanted to be recognized as speaking for God.

Feelings of jealousy are part of being human. Like all feelings, they are not wrong in themselves. It is the poor *choices* we sometimes make based on negative feelings that are wrong.

How has your life been affected by feelings of jealousy?

God of our struggles, help me be at peace with my gifts and talents. May jealousy never cloud my vision.

- To go deeper: Read Numbers 12:1–16.

Miriam: A Brother's Plea for Healing

> When the cloud went away from over the tent, Miriam had become leprous, as white as snow. And Aaron turned towards Miriam and saw that she was leprous. . . . And Moses cried to the LORD, "O God, please heal her."
>
> (Numbers 12:10,13)

The feelings of jealousy toward Moses had so affected Miriam that she contracted leprosy. Rather than being grateful that Miriam had "gotten hers," Moses pleaded with God to heal her. One can only imagine what feelings must have stirred up within Miriam. Her brother, against whom she had spoken, not only forgave her, he prayed for her to be healed! Prayer healed Miriam of her jealousy and of her leprosy.

Is there someone in your life whom you are jealous of? Is there someone who is jealous of you? Can you pray for that person?

Compassionate One, grant that I may turn to you in prayer when I am overcome by feelings of jealousy or when I am aware that someone is jealous of me.

• To go deeper: Read Numbers 12:1–16.

Miriam: Stepping Back

So Miriam was shut out of the camp for seven days; and the people did not set out on the march until Miriam had been brought in again.

(Numbers 12:15)

Like all of us, Miriam had to live through the consequences of her choices. In the heat of jealousy, she had spoken against her brother and now suffered leprosy. The law required she be separated from the group for seven days. It was not a permanent separation, but rather a reflective one. Her people even waited for her before they moved on—surely a sign of how much she was loved.

Times of stepping away from the group are important, especially during the teen years. Time away allows us to reflect on the choices we have made and the direction we are taking. We can take these breaks knowing that the people who love us will be there, waiting for our return.

What have you learned from times when you have stepped back from your friends?

Teach me, Lord, to recognize the times when I need to step back from my friends. Give me a reflective heart so I may grow stronger through the separation.

• To go deeper: Read Numbers 12:1–16.

Joshua: A Righteous Man

So the LORD said to Moses, "Take Joshua son of Nun, a man in whom is the spirit, and lay your hand upon him . . . commission him."

(Numbers 27:18–19)

Joshua's name means "Yahweh saves." He was Moses's successor, who was commissioned to lead the Israelites into the Promised Land. Joshua was known to be a righteous man and a courageous warrior. God was with Joshua just as God had been with Moses. Joshua led the Israelites across the Jordan River on dry land, just as Moses had led the Israelites across the Red Sea on dry land. Joshua also interceded with Yahweh on behalf of God's people and reminded them of their Covenant with God, just as Moses had done.

God expects each of us to be righteous people. Just like Joshua and Moses, we are called to follow God's Commandments and be an example to others.

How has your living God's Commandments influenced others around you?

God, your Commandments make us strong. May we continue to be led by them.

- To go deeper: Read Numbers 27:12–23.

Joshua: God's Promise

> Do not be frightened or dismayed, for the LORD your God is with you wherever you go.
>
> (Joshua 1:9)

Joshua was promised God's constant presence in his life if he would do but one thing—meditate upon the laws revealed to Moses day and night and then act in accordance with the laws. God revealed to Joshua that this was the path to success. God was not concerned about Joshua's skill in battle or his courage in difficult situations, but God was concerned about Joshua's faithfulness to God's Law. The Commandments provided all the direction Joshua would need.

Each of us has specific talents and skills we excel at, or admirable qualities that others affirm in us. However, just as with Joshua, God desires that we stay focused on God's Commandments. Our personal gifts and qualities are assets that help us act in accord with God's laws.

As you reflect on the Commandments of God, what gives you strength to lead a righteous life?

God, help me meditate upon your holy Commandments and follow them at all times.

- To go deeper: Read Joshua 1:1–9.

Joshua: Rahab Lends a Helping Hand

Now then, since I have dealt kindly with you, swear to me by the LORD that you in turn will deal kindly with my family.

(Joshua 2:12)

Rahab, a woman from Jericho, gave safety to two Israelite spies that were sent by Joshua to gather information before they crossed the Jordan River. Rahab helped the spies escape by lowering them with a rope from the window of her home that was partially outside the city wall. In exchange, Rahab asked that she and her family be given safety when Israel attacked Jericho.

Threats against our safety may take different forms today. Drugs, gangs, or gossip can all destroy people's lives. Like Rahab, we can be people who help others escape their destructive power. We might find ourselves being rescued in return.

Have you ever been asked to be an ally for someone who has felt threatened? What was your response?

God, you use the most unlikely allies in my life to keep me safe. May I always recognize your face in theirs.

- To go deeper: Read Joshua 1:1–24.

Joshua: Entering the Promised Land

> While all Israel were crossing over on dry ground,
> the priests who bore the ark of the covenant of
> the LORD stood on dry ground in the middle of the
> Jordan.
>
> (Joshua 3:17)

The Israelites crossed the Jordan River on dry land, led by
the ark of the Covenant, a sacred chest holding the Ten
Commandments Moses received on Mount Sinai. When
the entire nation had crossed, and the memorial of twelve
stones was erected, the priests finished carrying the ark
across the Jordan, and the river once again flowed as it
had before. The Israelites, led by God's Commandments,
were filled with confidence and promise as they entered
the Promised Land.

We, like the Israelites, are filled with confidence and
promise when our lives are guided by the laws of God.
Just as Joshua was exalted because of his righteousness,
those who follow God's Commandments will be exalted.

When have you been affirmed for simply following
God's Commandments?

*God, your Commandments lead me to the fullness of
life I long for. Help me to keep them.*

• To go deeper: Read Joshua 3:1–17.

Joshua: Conquering the Promised Land

> Joshua took all these kings and their land at one time, because the LORD God of Israel fought for Israel.
>
> (Joshua 10:42)

After the Promised Land was in the possession of the Israelites, Joshua divided up the land between the various tribes of Israel. Each tribe settled in its given area. To mark their victory, Joshua summoned all of Israel's leaders to Shechem to renew their Covenant with God and erect a memorial there. As they went forth to the various regions of the Promised Land, Joshua urged the Israelites to remain faithful to Yahweh.

Just as each tribe of Israel was given a particular place in the Promised Land to live out its faithfulness to God, each of us has been put in a specific place at a particular time in history to make known God's faithfulness to those around us.

How do you live your faith in your family, your school, and your community?

Good and generous God, thank you for placing me in the world today to be your witness.

- To go deeper: Read Joshua 23:1 — 24:1.

Joshua: Renewing the Covenant Commitment

"As for me and my household, we will serve the LORD."

(Joshua 24:15)

Joshua urged the Israelites to always remember that God is the surest hope in all the ups and downs of life. Joshua's last challenge to his people was to revere God and serve God sincerely and faithfully by getting rid of any of the other gods they had brought along from the past. Joshua emphasized that they have to choose whom they will serve—Yahweh or some other god. Joshua made it clear that he had chosen to serve Yahweh.

The same question is true for us today. We have to decide whether we will serve God or some other thing that has become a god—money, fame, and so on. It is no easier choosing God today than it was for Joshua. Keep in mind what Joshua knew to be true—that God is our surest hope.

How will you respond to Joshua's challenge: "Choose this day whom you will serve" (24:15)?

God of hope, may I always choose to serve you, for you are steadfast and faithful.

- To go deeper: Read Joshua 24:14–28.

Joshua: Death of Joshua

"After these things Joshua son of Nun, the servant of the LORD, died, being one hundred ten years old."

(Joshua 24:29)

Joshua lived a long life in the service of God. The Bible records that he was one hundred and ten years old when he died. A long life was the writer's way of telling us that Joshua was a man who had a right relationship with God. Throughout his life, Joshua had one goal, and that was to lead the people of Israel in the way of God's Commandments. Joshua's strength, his ability to lead the Israelites, was in his faithfulness to God.

Who in your life have been examples of faithfulness to God? How have their faith-filled lives enriched your own? As you examine their lives of witness, what faith qualities do you wish to incorporate into your life?

When you die, what will be said about your faithfulness to God?

God, thank you for the people who inspire me by their faithfulness to your commands.

- To go deeper: Read Joshua 24:29–33.

Deborah: The Deliverer

> [Deborah] sent and summoned Barak . . . "The LORD, the God of Israel, commands you, 'Go, take position at Mount Tabor.'"
>
> (Judges 4:6)

Following the death of Joshua, a gifted group of leaders emerged among the tribes of Israel. Referred to as Judges, they were a mix of warrior, religious leader, and defender of rights. One of the most prominent of these judges was the prophet Deborah. A woman's delivering a message from God and directing an army commander was very unusual. But Deborah provided the courage her people needed to defeat their enemy, the Canaanites.

God often speaks to us through those we least expect. It is a tribute to the Israelites that they heeded Deborah's message from the Lord. Listening to God's message from an unexpected source requires a lot of trust.

Who or what in our world today seems to be speaking for God?

God of surprises, open the ear of my heart to hear you speaking, even through unexpected messengers.

- To go deeper: Read Judges 4:1–23.

Deborah: Belts Out a Ballad

Deborah and Barak son of Abinoam sang on that day, saying . . . "So perish all your enemies, O LORD! But may your friends be like the sun as it rises in its might."

(Judges 5:1,31)

Often stories of heroic feats are set to music. We call them ballads. Deborah and Barak, victorious in battle against their enemies, the Canaanites, sang a prayer ballad. Their enemies were God's enemies, and through the power of God, Deborah and Barak defeated them. Their delight caused them to break out in song.

Through music we are able to express our deepest feelings and desires. This is especially true for young people, who often turn to music to express their feelings. Many popular musicians challenge the enemies of goodness today—war, alienation, and poverty. May our voices rise in song to God, and may justice and peace shine on all people.

What themes are addressed in the music you listen to regularly?

Place a song of peace in my heart, God, that I may help justice rise anew each day.

• To go deeper: Read Judges 5:1–31.

Gideon: The Reluctant Warrior

> Gideon answered [the angel], "But sir, if the LORD is with us, why then has all this happened to us? And where are all the wonderful deeds that our ancestors recounted to us?"
>
> (Judges 6:12–13)

Gideon, another biblical judge, was called to save his people from their enemy, the Midianites. Hearing the angel proclaim that God was with him was difficult because Gideon equated God's presence with an enemy-free existence. Gideon complained that God had been with the people of the past, but that God was not with them now.

Comparing ourselves to others who seem favored by God is a temptation. It is easy to believe that God is with us in good times and to have our doubts in bad times. Like Gideon, we are called to believe that God is with us at all times.

When have you felt as though someone else was getting the better deal from God?

God of all goodness, you have worked in the lives of those who have gone before me. Help me see that you also work in my life.

• To go deeper: Read Judges 6:11–35.

Gideon: Testing God

> Gideon said to God, "In order to see whether you will deliver Israel by my hand, as you have said, I am going to lay a fleece of wool on the threshing floor."
>
> (Judges 6:36–37)

Most people do not like being tested. We are never really told how God felt about Gideon's test, but God probably did not like being tested either. Before Gideon would trust God's word, he needed proof. Gideon put God to the test. God passed, and Gideon went on to be victorious.

It is not uncommon to test our family members to see how much our parents and siblings love us or will do for us. Like Gideon, we want to know the extent to which our parents, teachers, and even God will be there for us. But God's love for us never needs to be tested. It is forever.

In your prayer, do you ever test God with sentiments such as, "God, if I pass this test or get this job, then I will know you love me"?

God, remind me that you do not need to prove yourself. Grant that I may accept you at your word.

- To go deeper: Read Judges 6:36–40.

Samson: Special Before Birth

"It is [Samson] who shall begin to deliver Israel from the Philistines."

(Judges 13:5)

The strength of Samson is legendary. Even before his birth, he was singled out to be a special judge of his people. As a Nazarite, Samson vowed to abstain from alcohol, avoid contact with dead bodies, and refrain from cutting his hair. Samson's God-given strength assisted him in his efforts to defeat the Philistines.

The teen years are a time for assessing one's God-given talents and determining what disciplines will be needed to cultivate those talents. Similar to Samson, young people are often asked to promise they will not drink alcohol. They are called to be disciplined as they begin to develop their God-given talents.

What are your God-given strengths? What disciplines are necessary to cultivate those strengths?

Lord of my life, thank you for the gifts, talents, and strengths you have given me. Grant me the discipline I need to develop them to their fullest.

• To go deeper: Read Judges 13:1–24.

Samson: An Eye for an Eye

> "Do you not know that the Philistines are rulers over us? What then have you done to us?" [Samson] replied, "As they did to me, so I have done to them."
>
> (Judges 15:11)

During the time of Samson, justice was governed by a certain sense of equality. A person who was injured by someone could injure that person in return, but only equal to the original victim's injury. The saying "an eye for an eye and a tooth for a tooth" reflects this mentality.

This mind-set influenced Samson's desire to get even with the Philistines. Even God's chosen leaders struggled with wanting revenge against their enemies. It is only natural to feel that way. But Jesus calls us to move beyond those feelings, and to let God's justice reign.

How strongly do you feel about wanting to get even with someone who has hurt you?

God of compassionate justice, rid my heart and life of wanting to get even with those who have hurt me. Help me rise above the need to retaliate.

- To go deeper: Read Judges 15:9–20.

Samson and Delilah: A Couple in Trouble

> After this [Samson] fell in love with a woman . . . whose name was Delilah. The lords of the Philistines came to her and said to her, "Coax him, and find out what makes his strength so great, and how we may overpower him."
>
> (Judges 16:4–5)

Samson fell in love with Delilah, and she didn't return his love. Delilah simply used Samson, and his love for her, for her own selfish purposes. Samson was pestered by Delilah to reveal the secret of his strength, which eventually he did. It led to his death.

Betrayal by a friend is not uncommon in life. The betrayals we experience most likely will not lead to physical death, as they did for Samson, but they can harm us emotionally and keep us from trusting again.

How have you handled situations of betrayal by those whom you thought were your friends?

God, my forever friend, keep me faithful in my friendships. If I am betrayed, help me trust again.

• To go deeper: Read Judges 16:1–31.

Ruth: A Foreign Bride

[Naomi's two sons] took Moabite wives.

(Ruth 1:4)

The Book of Ruth is one of the few books in the Bible named for and principally about women. Ruth is also a foreigner. The story of Ruth begins with a famine that drove a devout Jewish family (Elimelech, his wife Naomi, and their two sons) from Bethlehem to a bordering country. While there the two sons married women from Moab, one named Orpah and the other, Ruth. Tragically, all the men of the family died. Ruth refused to let Naomi return to her home country alone and went with her mother-in-law to care for her.

Ruth's devotion to Naomi and her faithfulness to Naomi's God went beyond what was expected of her. God rewarded Ruth for her faithfulness, and her name is listed among the ancestors of Jesus.

When have you gone above and beyond what was expected of you? How were you rewarded?

God, may I always be faithful to you and go beyond what is expected of me in helping those in need.

- To go deeper: Read Ruth 1:1–5.

Ruth and Naomi: Sacrificial Love

"Where you go, I will go; where you lodge, I will lodge; your people shall be my people, and your God my God."

(Ruth 1:16)

We aren't told why or how Naomi's husband and two sons died. But if she had stayed in this foreign land, uncertainty and poverty would have been her only future. At least the laws and customs of her own people provided some care and support for widows. So Naomi decided to return to Bethlehem. Ruth decided to follow Naomi, risking rejection in a foreign land and sacrificing her ties to her own family and culture by choosing to follow the God of Israel.

Immigrants today face rejection and sacrifice as they start a new life in a foreign country. You may have even had family members who were immigrants at one time. If so, do you know about the hardships they experienced?

What sacrifices do immigrants make in trying to start a new life?

God of changes, help me be sensitive to the difficulties and hardships of the immigrant families in my community.

• To go deeper: Read Ruth 1:7–18.

Ruth and Naomi: Grief and Hope

> So Naomi returned together with Ruth the Moabite, her daughter-in-law.
>
> (Ruth 1:22)

The family and friends of Naomi must have hardly recognized her when she returned to Bethlehem. The tragic losses of her husband and sons had to have taken their toll on her. And then there was the young, foreign woman who traveled with Naomi. Ruth was now a refugee in search of a home along with her mother-in-law.

How quickly life had changed for Ruth and Naomi. Both of them had to try to find their way through the grieving process and to adjust to life as widows. Ruth had to learn the language and the customs of the Hebrews. Fortunately, they had the help of Naomi's extended family.

Your teen years also have their share of challenges, which are always easier to bear when you have the support and help of others.

What challenges and changes have you experienced in the last few years? Who has helped you through those times of change?

God, be with me in times of loss and change. Give me hope when all seems hopeless.

• To go deeper: Read Ruth 2:1–8.

Ruth: Noticed by Boaz

"All that you [Ruth] have done for your mother-in-law since the death of your husband had been fully told me."

(Ruth 2:11)

Ruth had been working hard all day in the field where Naomi had told her to gather the leftover grain when Boaz, a kind man related to Naomi's family in Bethlehem, first noticed Ruth. Boaz could have just dismissed Ruth as another poor foreigner, but instead he took time to inquire as to who she was. Boaz was struck by Ruth's dedication and love for her mother-in-law, Naomi.

Boaz had the openness not to judge Ruth by her nationality or ethnic background, but by her actions. Although we all like to think we are without prejudice, it is alive and well in our culture. Moving past such judgments takes an open mind and an open heart.

When have you let someone's background prevent you from getting to know them better?

Lord, help me to not judge people by their cultural background and to take the time to get to know their true selves.

• To go deeper: Read Ruth 2:1–25.

Ruth: Loyal and True

[Boaz] said, "May you be blessed by the LORD, my
daughter; this last instance of your loyalty is better
than the first."

(Ruth 3:10)

One of the ways Jewish Law provided for young widows
was to give the widow's deceased husband's male
relatives the opportunity to marry her. When Ruth noticed
that Boaz was being extra kind to her, she told Naomi.
Naomi coached Ruth on just what she should do to let
Boaz know that she was interested in him as a husband.
Ruth did as Naomi had instructed and demonstrated her
loyalty to Boaz and to Jewish Law.

As a foreigner, Ruth was not obliged to follow Jewish
Law and could have certainly sought out a younger man
to marry. Ruth, however, recognized God's goodness in
Boaz, and God rewarded Ruth's loyalty.

When have you felt rewarded in choosing to do what
you knew was the right thing to do?

*Dear Lord, may I follow the example of Ruth and
Boaz and be a faithful friend to the people you place
in my life.*

• To go deeper: Read Ruth 3:1–18.

Ruth: Marriage to Boaz

> Then all the people who were at the gate . . .
> said, "We are witnesses. May the LORD make the
> woman [Ruth] who is coming into your house like
> Rachel and Leah, who together built up the house
> of Israel."
>
> (Ruth 4:11)

Seeing beyond their cultural differences, Boaz recognized
that Ruth shared his love for God's people and God's law
and desired to marry her. The marriage of Ruth and Boaz
was witnessed by God's people and opened the door
to a new life for Ruth. Now she and Naomi would have
a secure future. And Ruth's status among God's people
would be equal to other matriarchs of the Jewish faith who
had gone before her.

The story of Ruth illustrates that God's covenant of love
is open to all people. God calls us to overcome the things
that divide us by building bonds of love.

How can you help overcome the barriers that keep
people divided from one another?

*God of love, thank you for caring people who, by
their love, overcome the barriers that divide people.*

• To go deeper: Read Ruth 4:1–12.

Ruth: David's Great Grandmother

> When [Ruth and Boaz] came together, the LORD made her conceive, and she bore a son.
>
> (Ruth 4:13)

Imagine the joy Naomi experienced when she discovered that Ruth and Boaz were to have a child! A child restores any woman's hope in the future. Ruth gave birth to a son, Obed, who would ease the loss that Ruth and Naomi had experienced. Obed grew up in Bethlehem and eventually had a son named Jesse, who, in turn, became the father of David, the great king of Israel and ancestor of Jesus. Ruth is one of four women mentioned in Jesus's family tree (see Luke 1:5).

God's plan for good does not discriminate between race, creed, or color. The Son of God was born of a family tree that included saints and sinners, Jews and Gentiles, women and men, all people of God.

Who have been ancestors in faith for you—not necessarily relatives, but those who have shared their faith with you?

Thank you, loving God, for the people who have shared their faith with me.

- To go deeper: Read Ruth 4:13–22.

Samuel: Reluctant King Maker

"You [Samuel] are old and your sons do not follow in your ways; appoint for us, then, a king to govern us. . . . But the thing displeased Samuel."

(1 Samuel 8:5–6)

Samuel was the son of Elkanah and Hannah, born after Hannah had been childless for many years. Because God had answered her prayer, Hannah dedicated Samuel to God as a Nazarite—one who vowed not to drink alcohol or cut his hair. As a young boy, Samuel was taken by his parents to Shiloh, the place of the ark of the Covenant, to live at the temple, with the priest Eli as his mentor. Samuel became a great leader in Israel, first as a judge and then as a prophet. He anointed the first two kings of Israel—Saul and David.

Spiritual mentors serve an important purpose in our lives. They help us to recognize and respond to God's call.

Who is a spiritual mentor for you—someone who helps you recognize and respond to God's call?

God, when I hear your voice, let my response be like Samuel's: "Speak, LORD for your servant is listening."

• To go deeper: Read 1 Samuel 1:12–28.

Samuel: Child Favored by God

> "[God] will guard the feet of his faithful ones, but the wicked shall be cut off in darkness."
>
> (1 Samuel 2:9)

The Scripture quote above is the words of Samuel's mother, Hannah, in praise of God for giving her a son after being childless for many years. Her words are similar to the words prayed by Mary after she discovered she would be the mother of Jesus. Both women offered a prayer of thanksgiving to God because God had blessed them so richly. Both women understood that their sons would be instruments of God's goodness. The gratefulness of their hearts flowed over into spontaneous prayer.

God continues to show favor to us today. How has God blessed you in your life? How have you expressed gratefulness for those blessings in prayer?

What have your parents shared with you about the blessing of your birth and what they feel is God's plan for you?

God of favor, thank you for the many ways you have blessed me.

• To go deeper: Read 1 Samuel 2:1–10.

Samuel: Eli Teaches Samuel to Pray

"Samuel! Samuel!" And Samuel said, "Speak, for your servant is listening."

(1 Samuel 3:10)

Samuel, as a boy at Shiloh under the spiritual mentorship of Eli, slept in the temple of the Lord near the ark of the Covenant. One night Samuel heard a voice calling his name. Thinking it was Eli, he went to him, but Eli sent him back to sleep. After Samuel heard the voice calling three times, Eli instructed Samuel to respond in prayer. Eli taught Samuel how to be open to God, to be humble before God, and to hear what God was saying.

God speaks to us today, but often we do not recognize that it is God speaking. When you pray, remember to be open and humble enough to really listen to what God has to say.

Who has taught you to pray? How have they taught you to be open and humble so that you are able to take God's words to heart?

God, bless me with openness and humility so I will always be able to hear you speak to me.

• To go deeper: Read 1 Samuel 3:1–10.

Samuel: The Last Judge of Israel

"If you are returning to the LORD with all your heart, then put away the foreign gods."

(1 Samuel 7:3)

After the death of Eli, the Philistines continued to wage war against Israel. They even captured and carried away the ark of the Covenant. In response, God raised up Samuel as a judge. Samuel was to lead Israel against the Philistines and to bring the ark back home. As judge, Samuel called Israel to renew its Covenant with Yahweh: "Direct your heart to the LORD, and serve him only, and he will deliver you out of the hands of the Philistines" (1 Samuel 7:3).

Singleness of heart is what God asks of each of us. We cannot serve two gods. Samuel's advice is clear—direct your heart to God and only God. This isn't as easy as it sounds; our world has lots of distractions to tempt us away from God.

Where does God rank on your list of priorities? Is God first?

God, bring people of faith into my life to show me how to put you first in my life.

• To go deeper: Read 1 Samuel 7:3–17.

Samuel: Anointing Saul King

"The LORD has anointed you [Saul] ruler over his people Israel."

(1 Samuel 10:1)

Even though Samuel personally did not like the idea of having kings ruling over Israel, Samuel listened to God when he was told to heed the voice of the people. He warned the people about the dangers of kings as God directed him to. Then he allowed God to guide him in choosing Saul as the first king.

Sometimes it is difficult for us to listen to the voice of God speaking through others, especially when we have a different opinion. Samuel struggled with the people's desire for a king because it seemed like a rejection of God's rule over the people. Samuel resolved his struggle by taking everything to God in prayer and humbly listening to God.

What great struggle have you taken to God in prayer? What insights have you gained in listening to what God has to say to you?

God, sometimes it is so hard to find the right path to take. Help me discern your will.

- To go deeper: Read 1 Samuel 9:15—10:1.

Samuel: Anointing David as King

"Rise and anoint him [David]; for this is the one."
Then Samuel took the horn of oil, and anointed him
in the presence of his brothers.

(1 Samuel 16:12–13)

Because Saul rejected God's commands, God directed
Samuel to seek out a new king. God guided Samuel to
the house of Jesse in Bethlehem. Jesse presented seven
of his sons to Samuel, but Samuel knew God had not
chosen any of them. Samuel asked Jesse if any of his sons
were missing. Then Jesse sent for the youngest son, David,
who was tending the sheep. When David arrived, God
revealed to Samuel that David was the one to anoint as
king of Israel.

God has great plans for each of us. God calls us to use
our unique gifts and talents in the service of others. But it
helps to have individuals like Samuel show us how God
wants us to use our talents.

Who has been helpful in pointing out and encouraging
you to use your talents?

*God, help me encourage other people to use their
gifts for your purposes.*

• To go deeper: Read 1 Samuel 16:1–13.

Samuel: Death of Samuel

Now Samuel died; and all Israel assembled and mourned for him. They buried him at his home in Ramah.

(1 Samuel 25:1)

After a long life in the service of God, Samuel died and was greatly honored by all of Israel. Samuel was known for his openness to the will of God, which he learned from Eli as a boy. Because of Samuel's close relationship with God, he gained two important insights into what it means to be faithful to God. First, God wants us to obey the Commandments and not get overly concerned with ritual sacrifice. Second, God is concerned with what is in the human heart, not with outward appearances.

God knows our heart, and it is there that God wants to find goodness. Pious acts and outward appearances are no more than a facade if righteousness does not come from within.

What is at the very core of your being? When God examines your inner being, does God find a righteous person?

God of righteousness and truth, create in me a heart that is true to you.

• To go deeper: Read 1 Samuel 15:22, 16:7.

Saul: First King of Israel

> But the people refused to listen to the voice of Samuel; they said, "No! but we are determined to have a king over us."

> (1 Samuel 8:19)

Although Samuel had listened to God and had led the people of Israel wisely, the people had grown dissatisfied with the corrupt government of Samuel's sons. The people saw that the nations around them prospered under the leadership of a king, and they wanted a king as well.

God gave in to the people's request and told Samuel to anoint Saul king. But the people would soon find out that life under a king would bring its own hardships. Saul's reign would be a stormy one. Rather than listen to God as Samuel did, Saul thought God's law didn't apply to him, and he abused his position as king. His reign would eventually end violently.

Have you ever gotten what you wanted only to find out you were worse off than before?

Dear God, when I ask for things that might not be good for me, just ignore me, okay?

• To go deeper: Read 1 Samuel 8:1–22.

Saul: Who Me?

> Saul answered, "I am only a Benjaminite, from the least of the tribes of Israel."
>
> (1 Samuel 9:21)

When Samuel informed Saul that God had chosen him as ruler over God's people, Saul responded with disbelief. Saul was a small-town boy from a little-known family. He could not fathom why God would choose him from among all the men of Israel. When Samuel finally brought the tribes together to proclaim Saul king, Saul was found hiding among some baggage.

God had faith that Saul could do the job, but Saul was reluctant to do God's will. We may be just as reluctant when asked to assume a leadership position or to do a task that we don't feel qualified to take on.

When have you felt unsure about yourself or reluctant to take on a leadership position?

God, I am not always confident about my own abilities, and sometimes I am tempted to hide instead of trying something new. Give me the courage I need to take risks.

• To go deeper: Read 1 Samuel 9:15 — 10:24.

Saul: Victorious King

> When Saul had taken the kingship over Israel, he
> fought against his enemies on every side . . .
> and rescued Israel out of the hands of those who
> plundered them.
>
> (1 Samuel 14:47–48)

King Saul was a brave warrior, and he led the people of
Israel to many victories. Saul and his sons fought valiantly
alongside the army against neighboring tribes. Saul's
victories meant prosperity for Israel, and he was praised
as a successful warrior. His victories, however, would
be short-lived. Saul's unwise decisions and rejection of
what God had asked of him would eventually lead to his
downfall.

Positions of leadership often come with the privileges of
power, fame, and success, but there is also the temptation
to think ordinary laws don't apply to you.

What positions of leadership have you held? Were
you ever tempted to abuse your position by doing things
others weren't allowed to do?

*God of power, help me use positions of leadership to
serve others rather than for my own benefit.*

- To go deeper: Read 1 Samuel 14:47—15:10.

Saul: Tormented King

> Whenever the evil spirit from God came upon Saul, David took the lyre and played it . . . and Saul would be relieved and feel better.

> (1 Samuel 16:23)

Because Saul had gone against God's instructions, the spirit of God left him. Saul was now tormented by an inability to sleep, foul moods, and a violent change in his personality. David, one of Jesse's sons, was a skilled harpist and came to play for the king. David's music and his friendship had a healing effect on Saul.

Sleeplessness and mood swings are common experiences in the teen years and often are just a normal part of development. However, sometimes they can be signs of something more serious—like depression. Listening to music or hanging out with friends may relieve temporary bouts of moodiness, but when it turns to chronic depression, one needs to seek the help of family and professionals.

How do you find relief when you feel restless, moody, or depressed?

God, when I am feeling restless, moody, or depressed, calm me with your loving presence.

• To go deeper: Read 1 Samuel 16:14–23.

Saul: Jealous King

> [Saul] said, "They have ascribed to David ten thousand, and to me they have ascribed thousands; what more can he have but the kingdom?"
>
> (1 Samuel 18:8)

King Saul loved David. He relied on David's soothing songs and harp melodies to calm him. David was a loyal soldier. Saul's son, Jonathan, and David had become so close they were like brothers. But when the crowds began to acclaim David as a greater warrior than Saul, the king became insanely jealous!

Jealousy has a way of turning a loving relationship into one filled with hatred. It breeds suspicion, envy, and anger and can cause us to say and do hurtful things we may later regret. In the end, it can be more destructive to our own well-being than it is to others.

Have you ever been in or witnessed a relationship that turned ugly with jealousy? How did you or the other person control jealousy?

Lord, help me have realistic expectations of myself and others. Let me not be jealous of other people's accomplishments.

- To go deeper: Read 1 Samuel 18:6–30.

Saul: Repentant

> Then Saul said, ". . . I have been a fool, and have made a great mistake."
>
> (1 Samuel 26:21)

In his jealousy, Saul pursued young David and tried to kill him. One time Saul entered the very cave where David and his men were hiding. David and his men could easily have killed Saul. Instead, David secretly cut off a corner of the king's cloak to show Saul that he had spared Saul's life. It wasn't until David spared Saul's life a second time that Saul confessed his wrong and vowed never to harm David again.

Saul was so driven by jealousy and fear that David would take his position as king that he failed to recognize David's love and loyalty for him. When Saul finally did recognize how foolish he had been, he repented.

When have you let feelings of jealousy, anger, and hurt get in the way of seeing how much others love and care for you?

Merciful Lord, may I never act out of jealousy and anger and cause harm to another. Give me the courage to apologize when I do.

- To go deeper: Read 1 Samuel 24:1–16, 26:1–25.

Saul: Final Despair

So Saul took his own sword and fell on it.

(1 Samuel 31:4)

The First Book of Samuel ends with a tragic scene. The Philistines swarmed down upon Saul and killed his three sons and struck Saul with an arrow. Afraid of the torture and humiliation he would face in being captured by his enemies, Saul commanded his armor bearer to take his sword and kill him. The armor bearer refused to do what the king ordered. So, in total desperation, Saul killed himself.

Some people feel just as desperate as Saul and are tempted to take their own lives too. But suicide is never an answer to the sufferings life may bring. As long as you are alive, there is the possibility of things getting better. In times of despair, we must seek help from God and others.

Whom do you turn to when you are fearful and feeling hopeless?

Lord Jesus, help me put things in right perspective; let failure not lead me to despair; help me be faithful to the eternal hope you have won for us.

• To go deeper: Read 1 Samuel 31:1–13.

David: The Last to Be Chosen

> The LORD said, "Rise and anoint him; for this is the one."
>
> (1 Samuel 16:12)

When you are the last one chosen for something, it is easy to feel that you are just being tolerated. But in the Bible, God often chooses the people others would choose last because they are too young or too old, lacking ability, or just not seen as important. David, a young shepherd who was chosen by God to be king, is a prime example. Samuel thought one of David's older and more experienced brothers would be chosen as king, but God rejected all of them and chose David.

Our culture focuses heavily on outward appearances—having the right clothes, hairstyle, and so on—and places little value on inner qualities. God's choice of David illustrates that it is the goodness within that really matters to God.

Have you ever been the last one chosen for a group or team? Describe the experience and your feelings about it.

God, my creator, remind me often that you judge not by appearances but by the heart. Hold my heart close to you.

- To go deeper: Read 1 Samuel 16:1–13.

David: A Mighty Musician

"Let our lord . . . look for someone who is skillful in playing the lyre; and when the evil spirit from God is upon you, he will play it, and you will feel better."

(1 Samuel 16:16)

Music has the ability to express our deepest feelings and to release our inner moods. David, tradition tells us, had grown proficient as a musician during the many hours he spent tending his father's sheep. His musical talent became a gift to King Saul, who found that the notes carried away his spirit of sadness and dejection. Developing his God-given talent with music allowed David to bring comfort and peace to King Saul's troubled heart.

Each of us is responsible for discovering what talents God has given us. Music making is a talent many teens possess. Whatever your talent, God calls you to develop it for service to others.

How do you use music to express what you are feeling, to bring you healing and hope?

May you be praised, Lord, for the gift of music, which heals and soothes our weary hearts.

• To go deeper: Read 1 Samuel 16:14–23.

David and Jonathan: Friends for Life

> Then Jonathan made a covenant with David, be-
> cause he loved him as his own soul.

> (1 Samuel 18:3)

Aristotle, an ancient Greek philosopher, once said, "Friendship is a single soul dwelling in two bodies." This aptly describes the relationship between David and King Saul's son Jonathan. The two of them hit it off immediately and became friends forever. Their friendship was tested when Jonathan's father, King Saul, became jealous of David's military ability and popularity. Because David and Jonathan had established a covenant, Jonathan warned David of his father's plan and thus saved David's life.

Cultivating friendships is a vital experience of young people. As you continue to expand your horizons, do so by establishing bonds of friendship with those who share common interests, dreams, and hopes.

Who is your best friend? How has your friendship been tested?

God, thank you for the friends in my life. May my friends and I grow in our love and support of each other.

- To go deeper: Read 1 Samuel 20:1–42.

David and Bathsheba: A Tragic Flaw

> He saw from the roof a woman bathing; the woman was very beautiful. David sent someone to inquire about the woman.
>
> (2 Samuel 11:2–3)

As king, successful military leader, and married man, David was very blessed. But David wanted more—the beautiful woman, Bathsheba, whom he saw from his rooftop. David's desire for Bathsheba was so great that he had her husband, Uriah, sent to the front lines of battle and, ultimately, to his death. David's inability to be satisfied and grateful for his many gifts was his tragic flaw.

Think about all the commercials you see and hear every day. Aren't most of them saying that you need something more to be happy or fulfilled? An antidote for this desire to have it all is gratitude. A grateful heart helps us discipline our desires.

Has the desire for more ever caused you to do something you regret? What are you most grateful for?

Giver of all good gifts, grant me a grateful heart. May all my desires be directed to you.

- To go deeper: Read 2 Samuel 11:1–26.

David: Seeking Forgiveness

> David said to Nathan, "I have sinned against the Lord."
>
> (2 Samuel 12:13)

King David made choices that clearly were sinful. But because of God's mercy, that was not the end of the story. David chose to have an affair with a married woman, and he made arrangements for her husband to die in battle. Yet when David was confronted by Nathan the prophet with the evil he had done, David acknowledged his sin and in sorrow sought forgiveness from God. Despite his sinfulness, David sought to stay close to God.

Tradition tells us that David composed song-prayers called psalms. Through the Psalms, David sought pardon from God, asked God for what he needed, and praised God for his mercy and blessings. These ancient prayers have been used through the centuries and provide us with words to do the same.

When have you prayed the Psalms?

"Create in me a clean heart, O God, and put a new and right spirit within me" (Psalm 51:10).

- To go deeper: Read 2 Samuel 12:1–13, Psalm 51.

David and Absalom: Ever His Son

> [David] said, "O my son Absalom, my son, my son Absalom! Would I had died instead of you, O Absalom, my son, my son!"
>
> (2 Samuel 18:33)

Losing a child is a devastation that deeply affects parents forever. David was no exception. Even though Absalom had tried to kill David and make himself king, David was inconsolable when his soldiers killed Absalom. David's deep parental love for Absalom, no matter what he had done, illustrates the deep parental love that God had for his people.

It can be easy to fight with our parents or even hurt them with our words. When that happens, it can be difficult to believe that our parents, or God for that matter, can love and accept us. The story of David and Absalom serves as a reminder of God's unfailing love and forgiveness.

When have you felt your parents or God loving you despite what you have done?

God, my loving parent, remind me that you hold me in your heart always, no matter what I have done.

• To go deeper: Read 2 Samuel 18:19—19:8.

David: Declaring His Deliverer

David spoke to the LORD the words of this song on the day when the LORD delivered him. . . . He said: "The LORD is my rock, my fortress, and my deliverer."

(2 Samuel 22:1–2)

Pogo, a cartoon figure of years gone by, once joked, "We have met the enemy, and he is us." It is true. We are often our own worst enemy. Young people can be especially hard on themselves when they face their own inabilities and limitations. Turning to the Lord when this happens, as David did, can help us find the self-acceptance we need. The Lord will not necessarily take away our enemies—Saul continued to pursue David—but the Lord will give us insight, courage, and strength to face them. We only have to lean on the Lord, who is our rock, fortress, and deliverer.

When have you experienced the Lord bringing a rock, a fortress, or a deliverer in your life?

May you be the one to whom I turn, Lord, whenever I am in need of deliverance, support, or protection. Keep me from being my own worst enemy.

• To go deeper: Read 2 Samuel 22:1–51.

Solomon: The Third King

> There [at Gihon] the priest Zadok took the horn of
> oil from the tent and anointed Solomon.
>
> (1 Kings 1:39)

Solomon, the son of David and Bathsheba, succeeded David as the third king of Israel. Solomon's forty-year reign was considered Israel's golden age. It was a time of unprecedented stability and national unity. Solomon had a highly organized government, constructed magnificent buildings, and accrued much wealth. Yet it is the wisdom with which Solomon dispensed justice that makes him famous. Because of the stability of Solomon's reign, Israel did not have to expend its energies fighting wars and could devote itself to writing enlightened pieces of literature, which we call wisdom literature.

What legacy do you hope to leave to future generations after you die?

God, long after my death, may I be remembered as much for who I am as for what I did.

- To go deeper: Read 1 Kings 1:11–40.

Solomon: Rise to Power

> King [David] swore, saying, "As the Lord lives,
> . . . '[Bathsheba's] son Solomon shall succeed me
> as king.'"
>
> (1 Kings 1:29–30)

Solomon was aware God had chosen him to succeed David and to become king of Israel. David announced that Solomon was to succeed him as king in an oath sworn before God, even though Solomon was not David's oldest son. In a sense, Solomon's becoming king proved again that God's ways are not human ways.

It is good for us to recognize that we also have been chosen by God. We may not have been given any special advantage in a worldly sense, but God knows our potential for goodness and has chosen us to bring about God's Reign on earth.

When have you felt that God has chosen you to take on a role you do not feel qualified to take on?

God, I know that in your eyes I am important and of great value. Help me always remember this as I strive to carry out your will in my life.

• To go deeper: Read 1 Kings 1:38 — 2:9.

Solomon: Gift of Wisdom

> Give your servant therefore an understanding mind
> to govern people, able to discern between good
> and evil.
>
> (1 Kings 3:9)

In prayer, Solomon asked God for the gift of wisdom. God was pleased with his request and also gave Solomon riches and honor. Solomon's wisdom was best demonstrated in the story of the two women who both claimed to be the mother of the same baby. When Solomon called for a sword to divide the child between the two women, the real mother agreed to give up the child. Solomon knew the real mother would do whatever was necessary to keep her child alive.

Praying for wisdom not only makes a difference in our lives, but it can also make a difference in the world when we pray for wise leaders who will make decisions that foster justice and peace.

Have you asked God for the wisdom necessary to discern the many challenges in your life? Why or why not?

God, give me a wise heart, as you did to Solomon, so that I can serve the needs of others.

- To go deeper: Read 1 Kings 3:1–15.

Solomon: Building a Temple

> So I [Solomon] intend to build a house for the name of the LORD my God.
>
> (1 Kings 5:5)

Solomon built the first Temple in Jerusalem. He set out in earnest to complete this Temple so that the ark of the Covenant, which held the Ten Commandments, could reside there. It took seven years to complete the construction. Solomon used the best materials and employed the work of many, including the special architectural skills of the Phoenicians. Solomon's Temple remained standing for about 374 years, until it was destroyed by the Babylonians in 587 BC.

As Christians, we talk about our bodies being temples of the Holy Spirit. When we keep our bodies strong and healthy, we are honoring God and ourselves, because we are created in the image and likeness of God.

How do you give honor to God? How do you live out the Ten Commandments?

God, I long to give you honor and glory. Help me show respect and care for myself as well as for others.

• To go deeper: Read 1 Kings 5:1–18, 6:1–22.

Solomon: King for Forty Years

Thus King Solomon excelled all the kings of the earth in riches and in wisdom.

(1 Kings 10:23)

King Solomon was revered as a great king not only by the Israelites but also by the kings and queens of surrounding kingdoms. Dignitaries came from the ends of the earth to seek the wisdom of Solomon. In gratitude for his consul, the visitors gave Solomon riches of many kinds, from gold and silver to horses. Solomon was respected by his peers and those he ruled over.

Solomon was respected because of his great wisdom and justice. He gained the esteem of his peers and subjects by always being fair and just with them. We also want the respect of others. But we sometimes let our own motives and desires get in the way of treating others as fairly as we would want them to treat us.

How are you fair and just in your relationships with family and friends? Does this gain you respect?

God, teach me how to be fair and just with everyone I meet.

• To go deeper: Read 1 Kings 10:1–29.

Solomon: His Great Sin

> For when Solomon was old, his wives turned away his heart after other gods; and his heart was not true to the LORD his God.
>
> (1 Kings 11:4)

Even though Solomon was a great king, late in his life he allowed his foreign wives to lead him away from Yahweh. Solomon failed to do what God had required of him. Because Solomon disregarded God's Commandments, disunity broke out among the various tribes of Israel. As a result, Solomon's kingdom was split in two after his death.

All believers are required to remain faithful to God throughout their lives. In his old age, Solomon let other influences turn him away from God, even though he was a great and wise person. It is always a temptation to let material things or other people's approval get in the way of our relationship with God.

What influences in your life have the potential for leading you away from God?

God, may the good life you have given me never distract me from my relationship with you. Help me to remain faithful and to love you my whole life.

- To go deeper: Read 1 Kings 11:1–13.

Solomon: The Kingdom Splits

> Solomon slept with his ancestors and was buried in the city of his father David; and his son Rehoboam succeeded him.
>
> (1 Kings 11:43)

After forty years as king of Israel, Solomon died. Solomon's oldest son, Jeroboam, returned from Egypt, after having rebelled against his father, and rallied the ten northern tribes around him. Rehoboam, the son who succeeded Solomon as king, refused to listen to the demands of the northern tribes that found the burdens of taxes and forced labor too much to bear. This caused the tribes to split, with Jeroboam ruling the northern kingdom of Israel and Rehoboam ruling the southern kingdom of Judah.

Because Rehoboam was unable to be more compassionate and listen to the needs of the people, the kingdom split in two. Division often happens when the needs of individuals and groups are disregarded.

What conflicts and divisions exist today because people refuse to listen to one another?

God who heals divisions, help me to be compassionate and to listen to the needs of others.

• To go deeper: Read 1 Kings 12:1–33.

Tobit: Faithful and Observant Jew

> I, Tobit, walked in the ways of truth and righteousness all the days of my life.
>
> (Tobit 1:3)

Written during the Jewish Exile in Assyria, the Book of Tobit is a story—probably fictional—of one family's profound experience of God guiding their lives and intervening in times of suffering and humiliation. Tobit and his family were pious Jews who lived according to God's laws. They observed all the customs, prayers, and holidays of the Jewish people. Tobit taught his young son Tobias to respect all people, especially those in exile like them.

Families often pass on the customs and beliefs of not only their heritage but also their faith by adhering to certain traditions. Some traditions we look forward to celebrating each year, and others lose their meaning over time.

Which family traditions are meaningful for you and which are not?

God, help me appreciate the traditions of my family and faith community. Give me the wisdom to know which ones I should hold on to and which ones I can let go.

• To go deeper: Read Tobit 1:1–13.

Tobit: Defiant in the Face of Persecution

> I [Tobit] performed many acts of charity. . . . I would give my food to the hungry and my clothing to the naked; and if I saw the dead body of any of my people . . . I would bury it.
>
> (Tobit 1:16–17)

Even in exile, Tobit and his family tried to observe Jewish laws and customs. In defiance of the law of the king of Assyria, which allowed the dead to lie in the streets as a warning, Tobit insisted on secretly burying the dead. When the king discovered what he was doing, Tobit had to flee. He lost everything except his wife and son. Only the death of the king allowed Tobit to return to his family.

Tobit was faithful to God's law despite the dangers. Doing what we know is right is not always easy. It may require standing up for others when it is not the popular thing to do.

Who in our time continues to do what is right even if it costs them their freedom?

God, give me the courage to speak the truth and to do what I know is right.

• To go deeper: Read Tobit 1:16—2:7.

Tobit: Disheartened

> [Tobit] went to physicians to be healed, but the more they treated [him] . . . the more [his] vision was obscured.
>
> (Tobit 2:10)

One night while Tobit was sleeping outside, some bird droppings fell into his eyes. This caused a strange white film to form over his eyes, eventually causing blindness. Once a noble, wealthy, pious Jew, Tobit was gradually reduced to an angry, blind, and fumbling old man. He became suspicious of everyone, was depressed, and openly prayed to die.

Tobit sought physical healing, but his blindness went far deeper than just losing his eyesight. He had given in to despair and could not envision life ever getting better. Depression is common after experiencing a great loss, but we need to remember that God is always with us, especially in times of suffering.

Have you or has anyone you know suffered depression or been at the point of despair?

God, be with me in times of suffering, and don't let me give in to despair. Give me the strength to be your healing hands and to relieve the suffering of others.

- To go deeper: Read Tobit 2:9—3:6.

Tobit: Last Will and Testament

> "Revere the Lord all your days, my son. . . . Do not turn your face away from anyone who is poor, and the face of God will not be turned away from you."
>
> (Tobit 4:5,7)

Expecting to die soon, Tobit sent for his son, Tobias, and gave him instructions on how to live faithfully to God's law. Recalling that he had left some money in the far-off land of Media, Tobit decided to send his son on a journey to get it. Tobit was not only concerned that his family have enough money to survive but also that his son carry on the work of providing for the poor.

In a sense, Tobit was leaving his son his last will and testament. He was handing on his most valuable possession to his son—his faith in God. Most parents are concerned about passing on the values they have inherited from past generations to their own children.

What values or advice do your parents or grandparents want to pass on to you?

Dear God, open my heart so I can hear the wisdom you want to share with me through my family.

- To go deeper: Read Tobit 4:1–21.

Tobit: Guardian Angel

Tobit said to her, "Do not worry . . . for a good angel will accompany [Tobias]; his journey will be successful, and he will come back in good health."

(Tobit 5:21,22)

Before Tobit sent his son on the difficult journey into a foreign land, he told his son to find a trustworthy traveling companion. Tobias found a guide who was familiar with the roads and brought him to his father for his approval. Unknown to Tobit or his son, Tobias, the guide was really the angel Raphael, whom God had sent to watch over Tobias and to bring healing to Tobit.

Tobit and his wife were naturally concerned for the safety of their son. Even though they did everything possible to assure a safe journey, they knew things could happen that were beyond their control. Ultimately they had to entrust their son to God's care.

When have your parents worried about your safety? Have you ever been in a situation where you sensed that an angel was watching over you?

Protect and watch over me, Lord, as I journey through life.

• To go deeper: Read Tobit 5:1—6:1.

Tobit: Faithful Relationships

> "Marry a woman from among the descendants of your ancestors; do not marry a foreign woman . . . for we are descendants of the prophets."
>
> (Tobit 4:12)

As a good parent, Tobit was concerned that his son marry someone who would be faithful to God and to the traditions of God's people. When Tobias and Raphael arrived at the home of Tobit's relative in Media, Raphael encouraged Tobias to marry his kinsman's daughter, Sarah, according to his father's wishes. Tobias fell in love with Sarah and they wed. On their wedding night, Tobias and Sarah prayed and asked God to give them a long life together.

It was only natural for Tobit to want the best for his son. God also wants the best for us and wants us to have relationships that strengthen our relationship with God.

Which of your human relationships strengthen your relationship with God?

Write a prayer for your dearest friend. Ask God to keep your friend from harm and evil.

- To go deeper: Read Tobit 6:10—8:18.

Tobit: Mission Accomplished

> [Raphael] said, "Take courage; the time is near for God to heal you, take courage."
>
> (Tobit 5:10)

The angel that God sent to accompany Tobias on his journey was also sent to bring healing to Tobit. During Tobias's journey, Raphael taught Tobit's son the medicinal qualities of a fish's entrails. Tobias not only used them to heal his wife, Sarah, of a demon that had entered her but also to heal his father, Tobit, of his blindness.

Although we are told that God answered Tobit's prayer (see 3:16) and that God would heal Tobit (see 5:10) at the beginning of the story, Tobit's sight is not actually restored until chapter eleven. Like Tobit, God often answers our prayers in God's own time and through people and in ways we least expect.

When have you received an answer to a prayer in a way or through someone you least expected?

Faithful God, may I never get discouraged in waiting for an answer to a prayer. Help me recognize your power and presence working in others.

• To go deeper: Read Tobit 3:16–17, 11:7–17.

Elijah: Declaring a Drought

"As the LORD the God of Israel lives, before whom I stand, there shall be neither dew nor rain these years, except by my word."

(1 Kings 17:1)

Heroes in folklore often come out of nowhere as they appear to perform their heroic feats. This pattern is also seen in salvation history. Elijah the prophet seemed to have no family and no past. As a prophet, he also had a mission from God. He was to go to King Ahab and declare that the land would experience a severe drought.

The world today is no stranger to the destruction of droughts. It seems the environmental impact of global warming is being felt in every part of the earth. Scientists may be modern prophets like Elijah, warning us that unless we take better care of our planet, we too shall have "neither dew nor rain."

In what ways are you striving to care for the earth?

Global God, who has commanded us to care for the earth, grant us a spirit of reverence, respect, and renewal for all of nature.

• To go deeper: Read 1 Kings 17:1–7.

Elijah: Be Not Afraid

> Elijah said to [the widow], "Do not be afraid."
>
> (1 Kings 17:13)

It is not uncommon for young people to feel that their lives are over because of some traumatic event. It may be because of some misunderstanding that took place with a friend, because a boyfriend or girlfriend has left them, or because they made a wrong choice and now face consequences.

Elijah's words, "Do not be afraid," gave the widow a glimmer of hope as she prepared for her death and the death of her son. The widow placed her trust in Elijah and shared the meager amount of food and water she had. Through her trust, the meal and oil were multiplied, and her life and the life of her son were spared.

When have life's circumstances left you feeling like your life was over? Who was your Elijah, telling you not to be afraid?

God of my life, may your love enfold me in those moments of despair when I need someone to remind me that you are near.

• To go deeper: Read 1 Kings 17:8–16.

Elijah: Make Up Your Mind!

"How long will you go limping with two different opinions? If the LORD is God, follow him; but if Baal, then follow him."

(1 Kings 18:21)

Someone once said, "not to decide is to decide." The prophet Elijah challenged the people to quit trying to have it both ways. They either believed God was God and followed God's laws, or they were followers of the pagan gods referred to as Baal. Each of us must also make this choice—either to follow God's ways or to follow the ways of the world, which conflict with God's laws. People today sometimes try to have it both ways too—following the gods of greed, dishonesty, lust, and pride during the week and then going to church on Sunday morning.

Recalling Elijah's challenge—to decide once and for all who we are choosing to follow—can direct us to follow God.

How do your choices show you are choosing to follow God? When do you try to have it both ways?

God of all our decisions, direct my heart to choose you and your way at all times and in all places.

• To go deeper: Read 1 Kings 18:1–36.

Elijah: The Sound of Silence

> [The angel] said, "Go out and stand on the mountain . . . for the Lord is about to pass by." . . . When Elijah heard [the sound of sheer silence], he wrapped his face in his mantle and went out and stood at the entrance of the cave.
>
> (1 Kings 19:11,13)

Impelled by a deep desire to find God, we may expect to find God in big and bold places rather than in the quiet and calm places of our lives. Elijah, when he was told to meet God on Mount Horeb, fell into this trap of expecting God in the grand and the glorious. When a wind came up, an earthquake took place, and a fire swept through, Elijah expected to find God. God was not to be found in any of these experiences. Elijah discovered God in the stillness of sheer silence. Noise abounds in our culture, especially in the lives of young people. Listening for God in silence is an art to be cultivated.

When have you heard God speak amid silent moments?

May I never fear the sound of silence, Lord, for I know it is then that you speak to me.

• To go deeper: Read 1 Kings 19:11–19.

Elijah and Elisha: The Spirit Lives On

> So [Elijah] set out from there, and found Elisha son of Shapat, who was plowing. . . . Elijah passed by him and threw his mantle over him.
>
> (1 Kings 19:19)

Following God's directive, Elijah set out from Mount Horeb and found Elisha plowing the field. Throwing his mantle, or cloak, over Elisha symbolized Elijah's spirit surrounding Elisha. Protected and fortified by this mantle, Elisha would carry forward the brave and bold spirit of prophecy that Elijah handed over to him.

Similar to someone being clothed with school spirit by wearing a letter jacket or school shirt, Elisha was called to Elijah's spirit of service to God by wearing Elijah's mantle. Elisha would learn from Elijah what it meant to be a prophet for the Lord.

What do you possess that represents carrying forward a treasured spirit?

God of the ages, show me how to best live out and hand on the Spirit you have given me.

- To go deeper: Read 1 Kings 19:19–21.

Elijah and Elisha: Concern for Others

Elijah said to Elisha, "Tell me what I may do for you, before I am taken from you." Elisha said, "Please let me inherit a double share of your spirit."

(2 Kings 2:9)

When people face death, their focus tends to be on themselves. Not so for Elijah. His concern was for his heir apparent, the prophet Elisha. For his part, Elisha knew what he needed from Elijah. Being filled with Elijah's spirit was not enough. Elisha wanted a double portion of Elijah's spirit.

The generosity of Elijah, whose concern was for Elisha, and the insightfulness of Elisha, who desired more than material possessions, are an inspiration for us. Amid the activities, responsibilities, and concerns of life, it is easy to neglect the simple question, "What may I do for you?" Those who most need to hear that question are often our family and friends.

Who in your life needs to hear you say, "What may I do for you?"

Lord my God, helper of all who need you, make me sensitive to the needs of others.

• To go deeper: Read 2 Kings 2:1–12.

Elisha: High Expectations

> Elisha sent a messenger to [Naaman] saying, "Go, wash in the Jordan seven times, and your flesh shall be restored and you shall be clean." But Naaman became angry and went away.

> (2 Kings 5:10–11)

Naaman, the commander of an army, suffered from leprosy. When Elisha sent word telling Naaman what he was to do in order to be healed, Naaman was offended. Naaman expected Elisha to come to him in person, call upon God for a cure, and wave his hand over the leprosy, which would then disappear.

The high expectations we have for events or people in our lives can leave us feeling angry if our expectations are not met. This can be especially true when we are sick and need God's healing. During those times, we need to trust that God is working, even if the situation does not make sense to us.

When have you been impatient with God and refused to do something that may have brought you healing?

Blessed are you, Lord my God, who works in my life in simple and straightforward ways.

• To go deeper: Read 2 Kings 5:1–19.

Judith: Bold Voice of Truth

"Who are you to put God to the test today, and to set yourselves up in the place of God in human affairs?"

(Judith 8:12)

The Book of Judith is the story—probably fictional—of a beautiful widow who showed that deep trust in God produces daring deeds. The other leaders of Judith's city of Bethulia had planned to surrender to the hated Assyrians if God didn't help them in five days. When Judith heard what the leaders had planned, she accused the city rulers of giving up even before they gave God a chance to prove God's greatness. Judith challenged the leaders to set an example by trusting in God.

When things are overwhelming, it is tempting to just give up and take the easy way out. Often injustices like bullying or abuse continue because people are too timid or terrified to challenge their leaders to take action.

When have you felt that leaders have not taken action to help those in need?

God of the powerless, give me courage to speak the truth and to challenge those in charge to act justly.

• To go deeper: Read Judith 8:9–29.

Judith: Beautiful and Courageous

> [Judith] made herself very beautiful, to entice the eyes of all the men.
>
> (Judith 10:4)

Judith fasted and prayed and asked God to use her beauty and intelligence to rescue her people. Carefully packing kosher food for herself and her maid in a pouch, she dressed in her most stunning outfit, and they left through the main city gate. The two walked directly into the enemy camp where they were, of course, captured and taken to General Holofernes. Judith's beauty and cleverness enabled her to convince Holofernes that she could help him gain an easy victory.

At first glance, Judith's story seems to perpetuate the stereotype that a woman's power is in her beauty. If we look deeper, we will see that Judith, a powerless widow in the eyes of her culture, trusted that God would use her completely—both mind and body—to accomplish God's will.

How open are you to letting God use your gifts for the good of others?

Dear God, help me to know myself better and to use my gifts to influence others for good.

• To go deeper: Read Judith 10:1–23.

Judith: Dead Drunk

> Judith was left alone in the tent, with Holofernes stretched out on his bed, for he was dead drunk.
>
> (Judith 13:2)

On the fourth day of her stay, Holofernes planned another dinner party during which Judith charmed Holofernes with her beauty and gracious manners. As others grew groggy, they staggered away to sleep off their drunkenness, leaving Judith and Holofernes alone in his tent. Holofernes, overcome with wine, passed out on his bed. Judith uttered a quick prayer for strength and approached the drunken general, stooped to take up his sword, and with two mighty blows cut off his head!

Unfortunately, our news often has stories of the terrible dangers that drunkenness (and drugs) lead to. The use of abusive substances has caused many to "lose their heads" and to act foolishly, even to the point of losing their lives.

Do you know anyone who has lost her or his life because of someone's drunkenness?

Compose a prayer for yourself and others who may be tempted by alcohol and drugs.

• To go deeper: Read Judith 12:10—13:8.

Judith: Victory Is Won

"May [God] reward you with blessings, because you [Judith] risked your own life when our nation was brought low, . . . walking in the straight path before our God."

(Judith 13:20)

Judith and her maid passed the Assyrian sentinels carrying their food pouch, which contained Holofernes's head, and freely walked into the night. Once back in Bethulia, Judith gave thanks and praise to God. A great victory celebration followed as they danced, sang, and offered hymns of praise to God, who had so strengthened Judith.

Judith was victorious over the evil threatening her life because she was faithful to God, even to the point of risking her life to save others. She did not claim this victory for herself, but gave credit and thanks to God in whom she had placed her complete trust.

Have you ever thought of thanking God when you achieve a huge goal?

Write a reminder to thank God for ideas, energy, and the spirit to do good. Put the reminder where you will see it regularly.

• To go deeper: Read Judith 15:14—16:17.

Esther: Savior of the Oppressed

Letters were sent . . . to all the king's provinces, giving orders to destroy, to kill, and to annihilate all Jews.

(Esther 3:13)

The Book of Esther is a story written to give hope to God's people who were living in foreign lands. Esther, a beautiful young Jewish woman, had become queen of the king of Persia. When Haman, the king's jealous assistant, convinced the king that the Jews did not obey the king and should all be killed, Esther, encouraged by her Uncle Mordecai, used her influence with the king to save God's people.

Anger, jealousy, and suspicion continue to fuel hatred among different people, religions, and nations today. It is often the people we least expect who are willing to stand up for the oppressed and marginalized; some contemporary women are Dorothy Day, Rosa Parks, and Mother Teresa.

What groups of people in your school or community are targets of suspicion or hatred?

God of all peoples, help me to look beyond the differences in others to see that everyone is loved by you.

• To go deeper: Read Esther 2:1—3:13.

Esther: Anxious and Fearful

Then Queen Esther, seized with deadly anxiety, fled to the Lord.

(Esther 14:1)

After Mordecai had convinced Esther she should go before the king, she was seized with fear, knowing that she risked being put to death in doing so. Esther turned to the Lord in fasting and prayer. After calling upon God to help, Esther went to the king. When the king saw that she was about to faint with fear, he assured her of his concern and asked what was troubling her. The queen composed herself and made a simple request—that the king and his assistant, Haman, attend a banquet she was giving that day in the hope of exposing Haman's evil plans.

Like Esther, sometimes we are asked to take risks and do something that may cause us great fear and anxiety. Esther knew she could not face her fears alone, so she called on God to help her.

What causes you great fear and anxiety? Have you turned to God to help you face your fears?

Lord God, help me face my fears, and don't let them keep me from helping others.

• To go deeper: Read Esther 5:3–8, 15:1–16.

Esther: Reward and Punishment

"See, I have given Esther the house of Haman,
and they have hanged [Haman] . . . because he
plotted to lay hands on the Jews."

(Esther 8:7)

At the banquet, King Ahasuerus asked Esther to tell him
what was troubling her. Queen Esther asked only that
her life and the lives of her people be spared because
she too was a Jew. When asked who had hatched the
plan against the Jews, Esther responded, "Haman." As
punishment, the king commanded that Haman be hung,
as Haman had planned to hang Mordecai.

The reality of our world today is that those who do
good are not always rewarded and those who do evil are
not always punished. However, the evil and good we do
does affect our lives, and God promises that our actions
will eventually be judged.

When have you seen the evil actions of someone
eventually destroy that person's own life?

*Just and merciful God, help me always make dec-
isions I will be proud of.*

- To go deeper: Read Esther 7:1—8:8, 16:1–17.

Amos and Micah: Prophets of Justice

Let justice roll down like waters, and righteousness like an ever-flowing stream.

(Amos 5:24)

Both Amos and Micah spoke out against the injustices practiced against the poor. Both prophets spoke of a universal morality, which demanded that humans practice God's justice. Amos directed his prophetic revelation against the corrupt kingdom of Israel under King Jeroboam II, but his words were not heeded. Micah directed his prophetic voice against the kings of Judah—Jotham, Ahaz, and Hezekiah. It was Hezekiah who heeded his words, and thus Judah was spared for a while.

Both Micah and Amos spoke words of justice directed at the kings of Israel and Judah, but their words are also relevant to our own lives. They show us God's passion for justice and fairness.

How do you champion the cause of poor people in your community today?

God of justice and fairness, let me hear the words of your prophets in a new way, so that I can be your justice in the world today.

• To go deeper: Read Micah 3:1–12.

Amos: Voice of the Poor

"I am a herdsman, and a dresser of sycamore trees, and the LORD took me from following the flock, and the LORD said to me, 'Go prophesy to my people Israel.'"

(Amos 7:14–15)

Amos was a poor shepherd and pruned trees for a living. Amos knew personally the suffering of the poor at the hands of the unjust policies of the kings, and it was out of this reality that God called Amos to be a spokesperson for God's justice.

Injustice has not been eradicated from our society today. Many injustices exist in our communities today—the poor often do not have access to the very basic needs required to sustain life. Or prejudicial attitudes cause discrimination against particular groups of people. God calls each of us to speak out against the injustices we encounter on a daily basis.

What injustice have you experienced personally or observed leveled against others in your community?

God, when I encounter injustice, give me the courage to speak out against it.

- To go deeper: Read Amos 2:6–16.

Amos: A Religion of the Spirit

Seek good and not evil, that you may live; and so the LORD, the God of hosts will be with you.

(Amos 5:14)

Amos preached that religion cannot be just going through the motions without any conviction of the heart. It has to be a religion of the spirit that first and foremost seeks the Kingdom of God and God's justice. This is where Amos saw hope for Israel. If the people of Israel once again listened and conformed their lives to God's word, God would bless them.

The people in the kingdom of Israel could not hear Amos's words because they were living the good life. They had so much that they were not concerned with those who had nothing. We too live in a very affluent society where we have so many things. The consequence of having too much is that we risk becoming completely absorbed in the good life.

What things in your life prevent you from hearing God's word?

God of blessing, I am grateful for all you have given me. May I in turn be generous with my neighbor.

• To go deeper: Read Amos 5:4–15.

Amos: The Voice of Truth

> Amaziah said to Amos, "O seer, go, flee away
> to the land of Judah, earn your bread there, and
> prophecy there."
>
> (Amos 7:12)

Amaziah, a prominent priest at Bethel, saw Amos as a threat. He sent word to King Jeroboam II that Amos was conspiring against the king, even though this was untrue, in the hope that Amos would be exiled. Amaziah succeeded in getting Amos exiled to Judah.

Truth is not always embraced by everyone, especially when it calls for significant change. Some people who have spoken the truth and suffered the consequences are Martin Luther King Jr. and Nelson Mandela. Being the voice of truth has its unique cost for each of us. However, it also has its unique reward. Your voice may be the very one needed to bring about change. The change may be immediate, or it may come about at a later time.

What truth are you called to speak even if it may cause you to be unpopular?

God, strengthen my heart so it will continuously seek the truth.

- To go deeper: Read Amos 7:10–17.

Micah: A Plea for Humanity

> Listen, you heads of Jacob and rulers of the house of
> Israel! Should you not know justice?
>
> (Micah 3:1)

Micah's message is a plea to restore social order, where neighbor cares for neighbor and all people are protectors of justice. In the Book of Micah, the author consistently speaks out against the savage unwillingness to respect the personal worth of one's neighbor, emphasizing that every person is made in the image and likeness of God. For Micah, good religion is an interior reality that is centered in God and manifested in good deeds.

Our God is passionate about justice. If there is no justice, then how can others come to know God? Micah called the kingdom of Judah to cease corrupt practices that robbed the poor of their dignity, and to recognize that each person has eminent value and worth as God's creation.

What policies and practices in our society today diminish the dignity of an individual?

God, help me to always see your image in each person I meet.

- To go deeper: Read Micah 3:1–12.

Micah: Messianic Hope

> But you, O Bethlehem of Ephrathah, who are one
> of the little clans of Judah, from you shall come forth
> for me one who is to rule in Israel.
>
> (Micah 5:2)

Embedded in Micah's call for societal reform was the ongoing hope that God would always be with Israel. Even though the Jewish people experienced dark days, God would never abandon them. Out of the smallest towns and the smallest clans, God would again restore Israel. Micah spoke of the remnant that would give rise to the new dawn when, once again, the people of Jacob would live in righteousness.

For Christians, Jesus is the new dawn that Micah spoke of—the Messiah sent by God to restore righteousness and justice. Each of us is also called to be a beacon of hope and light, especially in how we care for people who are poor and vulnerable.

How is hope evident in your life? What is the source of your hope? How do you give hope to others?

*God of hope, I trust that you will never abandon me,
even in the darkest of times.*

- To go deeper: Read Micah 5:1–9.

Micah: What Is Required?

> What does the LORD require of you but to do justice, and to love kindness, and to walk humbly with your God?
>
> (Micah 6:8)

Micah dedicated his life to helping others understand what God required of them. To stress his point, Micah criticized the wealthy landowners who oppressed the poor, the judges who handed down unfair judgments favoring the rich, and the false prophets who offered only a rosy picture in the shadow of pending destruction. For Micah, what God asked of his people was simple—to be a just people who loved completely and who always reverenced God.

God requires the same three things of us: to do justice, love kindness, and walk humbly with God. As you reflect on your own life, examine how these three virtues are present. List some concrete examples.

How do I do justice, love kindness, and walk humbly with my God?

God, I desire to do what you ask of me. Please give me the integrity to always be a person of justice, kindness, and humility.

- To go deeper: Read Micah 6:6–8.

Jonah: The Runaway Prophet

But Jonah set out to flee to Tar'shish from the presence of the LORD.

(Jonah 1:3)

Prophets are people chosen by God to remind others of God's demand to live good and faithful lives. The Book of Jonah is a tale about a prophet who was called by God to go and preach to Nineveh, a city known for its evil ways. Jonah, however, panicked at the thought of having to confront the people, and he ran in the opposite direction.

What Jonah felt and thought as he sought to avoid God's presence may be similar to what we experience at times: "Why do I always have to be the one 'chosen' to do the right thing?" "Why can't someone else go?" It can be especially difficult to have to confront your peers when they are doing something wrong. Wanting to run in the opposite direction is not an uncommon feeling.

How have you felt when you had to be the one to confront a peer or family member about doing the right thing?

Hold me in your presence, Lord, when I want to run from your call.

• To go deeper: Read Jonah 1:1–6.

Jonah: Flees into the Storm

> But the Lord hurled a great wind upon the sea, and such a mighty storm came upon the sea that the ship threatened to break up.
>
> (Jonah 1:4)

The decisions we make affect the lives of others. Jonah learned this only too quickly! In seeking to flee from God, he boarded a ship going in the opposite direction from Nineveh, where God had asked him to go. A sudden storm caught the ship, frightening its crew. Jonah's decision to run from God affected not only his life but also the lives of the sailors with him. The crew threw Jonah overboard, the storm ceased, and the sailors worshiped Jonah's God.

Our lives are full of opportunities to realize how our choices affect others' lives. Like Jonah, we are challenged to enter these storms and to know that God will be with us.

Amid life's storms, how have your decisions affected the lives of others?

Guide me, God, and help me to make good decisions, especially amid life's storms.

• To go deeper: Read Jonah 1:7–16.

Jonah: In a Whale of a Situation

> But the LORD provided a large fish to swallow up Jonah; and Jonah was in the belly of the fish three days and three nights.
>
> (Jonah 1:17)

Often in life we feel as though we are going from one tough situation to another. Perhaps it is conflict within the family, an illness, or maybe struggles at school or with friends. Having to go through a series of painful experiences can be overwhelming.

Jonah's tale of going from the storm into the stomach of the fish (sometimes called a whale) was a similar situation. He too felt overwhelmed. The symbolism of Jonah's being caught in the belly of the fish for three days relates to Jesus being in the tomb for three days. And just as Jesus (and Jonah in a sense) conquered overwhelming darkness and death by rising from the dead, so will we.

What situations in life have swallowed you up in a feeling of being overwhelmed?

God, my constant companion, help me turn to you when life seems to go from bad to worse.

• To go deeper: Read Jonah 1:17—2:10.

Jonah: Mad About Success

> When God saw . . . how they turned from
> their evil ways, God changed his mind about the
> calamity. . . . But this was very displeasing to
> Jonah.
>
> (Jonah 3:10—4:1)

Truly, God is a God of second chances. God spoke to
Jonah a second time and sent him to Nineveh to proclaim
God's message. This time Jonah obeyed, and his preaching inspired all its inhabitants to turn from their evil ways.
God relented and did not punish Nineveh. Jonah was
a success. He had fulfilled his mission, and yet he was
angry. Jonah felt the city of Nineveh should have been
punished for its wicked ways.

Teens are especially alert to fairness. It may seem very
unjust when two people commit the same offense but
receive different consequences. Unlike Jonah, we need to
rejoice when others experience mercy in their lives. We
need to let God be God.

When have you felt angry about someone's receiving
mercy instead of punishment?

*Merciful God, teach me to rejoice in the compassion
you offer others.*

- To go deeper: Read Jonah 3:1—4:11.

Hosea: Always Faithful

> The LORD said to me again, "Go, love a woman who has a lover and is an adulteress, just as the LORD loves the people of Israel, though they turn to other gods."
>
> (Hosea 3:1)

Hosea was a prophet, chosen by God, who lived what God asked him to preach. He lived in the northern part of the kingdom of Israel, where corrupt and unfaithful kings ruled the people of God. God asked Hosea to be an example of God's fidelity to the people, despite their unfaithfulness. Hosea was instructed to take back his wife Gomer, even though she had been unfaithful to him. Hosea was a living example of God's fidelity.

Faithfulness is a vital element of any relationship. Being faithful even when another betrays our fidelity makes us more godlike. This is the witness Hosea places before us.

How hard is it to be faithful to a friend, even when that person hasn't been a good friend to you?

Ever-faithful God, may your fidelity to me strengthen my faithfulness to you and others.

- To go deeper: Read Hosea 3:1–5.

Hosea: Counting on God

> Let us know, let us press on to know the LORD; his appearing is as sure as the dawn.
>
> (Hosea 6:3)

As human beings, we have a deep desire to know about others and to be able to rely on others. Hosea, the prophet of God, realized this. He called the people who were worshiping false gods to dedicate themselves to knowing more about the true God. Hosea wanted the people to realize they could count on God, who would always be there for them.

Our desire to know more about famous people has spawned major industries that keep us informed on what they say and do. People spend hours each week keeping up with the lives of these people. What would happen if we spent as much time coming to know more about God by reading the sacred Scriptures, the word of God?

In what ways do you dedicate yourself to knowing more about God?

Let me hear your word, Lord of my life, that I may come to know you.

- To go deeper: Read Hosea 6:1–11.

Hosea: See How Much God Cares

I led them with cords of human kindness, with bands of love. I was to them like those who lift infants to their cheeks. I bent down to them and fed them.

(Hosea 11:4)

It is amazing how many commercials employ babies or small children to sell their products. Most of us are naturally attracted to "little ones." Their innocence, enthusiasm, and vulnerability draw us to them. God uses this image of a tender relationship with children to communicate a message to Hosea. God tells Hosea, and us, that God is like a loving, caring parent who has compassion for the smallest and most vulnerable of God's people. The tenderness of God's care in these words to Hosea is meant to help God's people reflect on their response to such gentle affection and then return to God.

How have you experienced God's tender, loving care?

Tender God, as a loving parent, you seek to draw me closer to you. May I always lean on your love.

- To go deeper: Read Hosea 11:1–12.

Isaiah: God Is Salvation

> Do not fear, for I have redeemed you; I have called
> you by name, you are mine.
>
> (Isaiah 43:1)

Isaiah was one of the major prophets. His name means "God is salvation." He was born around 760 BC in the southern kingdom of Judah. Isaiah was an eager messenger of God, even though his messages often fell on deaf ears. The phrase "do not be afraid" is repeated time and time again in the Book of Isaiah.

Isaiah is remembered as a prophet of hope because his words, though challenging, brought consolation in difficult times. The words of Isaiah are still relevant today. During the season of Advent, we often read from the Book of Isaiah because he speaks of a future time when the Messiah will establish the Kingdom of God, and peace will reign. Christians believe Jesus fulfilled the words of the prophet Isaiah.

In your life, whose words both challenge you and help you to not be afraid?

God, Isaiah helps me understand that I do not need to be afraid, for you know me by name.

- To go deeper: Read Isaiah 43:1–13.

Isaiah: Empty Ritual

Wash yourselves; make yourselves clean; . . . cease to do evil, learn to do good.

(Isaiah 1:16–17)

Isaiah spoke out strongly in God's name against the empty rituals the Israelites practiced. They would go through the motions and do what was required by law, but practice idolatry and injustice in their everyday lives. Isaiah pointed out these hypocrisies and called Israel to once again be about living the commands of God—to do good, seek justice, and rescue the oppressed.

It is not uncommon to see someone piously attending church on Sunday morning and then intentionally doing something malicious or deceitful during the week. This is the kind of hypocrisy Isaiah spoke out against. Our prayer at church on Sunday has meaning only when we live our faith each day of the week. And when we live our faith each day, then our worship will be rich and fulfilling.

How is the way you live your faith daily consistent with what you proclaim on Sunday?

God, forgive me for the times when I have not lived the beliefs I proclaim in worship.

• To go deeper: Read Isaiah 1:10–20.

Isaiah: Be Nonviolent

> They shall beat their swords into plowshares, and their spears into pruning hooks; nation shall not lift up sword against nation.
>
> (Isaiah 2:4)

Isaiah called Israel to be a nation of peace, not one that wages war. He used the plowshare—the very sharp part of the plow that pierces the ground in order to turn it over in preparation for planting crops—as a symbol for peace. A nation that uses its resources for peace can raise food to feed the world, thus putting an end to hunger and injustice.

Pope Paul VI called those who want peace to work for justice. Too often violence is seen as the only answer when people or nations are in conflict. But violence is never a lasting answer to conflict. Isaiah and later Jesus taught another way—to love your enemies and work for a just end to conflict.

How can you support nonviolence in and through everything you do?

God, give me a heart only for peace so that when violence enters my life, I will know how to deal with it in a nonviolent way.

• To go deeper: Read Isaiah 11:1–9.

Isaiah: Here I Am

"Whom shall I send, and who will go for us? And [Isaiah] said 'Here am I; send me!' And [God] said, 'Go.'"

(Isaiah 6:8–9)

In a vision, Isaiah found himself before God, who was being attended to by angels. Aware of his sinfulness, Isaiah cried out that he was a man of unclean lips. Immediately one of the angels took a hot coal from the altar, touched Isaiah's lips, and blotted out his sins, thus making Isaiah ready to respond to God's call. Isaiah responded positively to God and embraced his role as a prophet, a spokesperson for God, to Israel. Isaiah was confident that God was calling him to prophesy to Judah.

We are also being called to bring God's message to the world. When we ready our hearts and embrace our mission fully, then God will be able to work through us to bring about changes in the world.

What is God calling you to do to bring about justice in the world?

God, give me ears to hear your call and conviction to embrace it completely.

• To go deeper: Read Isaiah 6:1–13.

Isaiah: Messianic Prophecy

"Therefore the Lord himself will give you a sign. Look, the young woman is with child and shall bear a son, and shall name him Immanuel."

(Isaiah 7:14)

Isaiah spoke words of hope to the Israelites; he prophesied a future when God would be with them once again, a time when the Covenant between God and the Israelites would be restored. The Israelites would know that time had arrived when a child named Immanuel—God with us—was born of a virgin (young woman, in some translations).

As Christians, we understand and believe that Jesus is the promised child, the Messiah, who bears the name Immanuel. Jesus is the fulfillment of God's Covenant. It is Jesus who came to call all people to follow the Commandments of God—to love God completely and to love your neighbor as yourself.

Who demonstrates love for God and others and serves as sign of hope for you?

God, you are hope for every generation. Show me how to bring others to that hope.

• To go deeper: Read Isaiah 7:10–25.

Isaiah: Trust in God

Surely God is my salvation; I will trust, and will not be afraid, for the LORD GOD is my strength and my might.

(Isaiah 12:2)

Isaiah's message was consistent—trust in God. This is the only sure thing in life. Even though trust may be violated in human relationships, our trust in God must never be diminished. It is hardest to place trust in God during times of great fear. Fear brings about distrust in ourselves, in others, and in God. Isaiah repeated over and over, "Do not be afraid, God is always with you."

If fear brings about distrust, then only love can bring about trust. The love of self, others, and God dispels fear. When fear is overcome, trust can flourish. If we embrace God's love and are God's love in the world, fear will have no foothold.

How do your fears keep you from trusting others and God?

God, I want to place all my trust in you; help me overcome my fears.

• To go deeper: Read Isaiah 12:1–6.

Isaiah: Servant of God

> Here is my servant, whom I uphold, my chosen, in whom my soul delights.
>
> (Isaiah 42:1)

Isaiah presents the idea of a servant leader, a leader who is a role model for those to whom they are sent. A servant leader is righteous, lives in accord with God's Covenant, and thus becomes a light for the whole world. Servant leaders are able to lead in such a fashion because God's Spirit lives within them, and they know God looks upon them with favor.

Jesus was the primary example of a servant leader. He put the good of others even before his own safety. When we lead by modeling goodness and kindness, we also are servant leaders. The challenge in being a servant leader is to not become discouraged, but to stay the course and be consistent. Our reward may come only from God.

Whom would you describe as a servant leader? What qualities of righteousness do you see in this person?

God, I pray that all leaders will follow Jesus's example of being a servant leader.

- To go deeper: Read Isaiah 42:1–9.

Jeremiah: Man of Visions

Then the Lord put out his hand and touched my mouth; and the Lord said to me, "Now I have put my words in your mouth."

(Jeremiah 1:9)

The Book of Jeremiah is a long collection of speeches that Jeremiah gave to the people of Israel. Jeremiah knew his country was about to be defeated in war because God's people were unfaithful. He warned the people of their coming fate through prophetic speeches and by symbolically acting out his visions. Even though many people knew Jeremiah was speaking the truth, they ridiculed and ignored him.

At times people who have special insights frighten us. For example, scientists have been warning us for years about the ways we are harming our environment. Even though we know they speak the truth, we often do not want to hear what they have to say because it means we will have to change the way we live.

What steps can you take to help reverse the damage we are doing to the planet?

God of all creation, help me heed the voice of modern prophets.

- To go deeper: Read Jeremiah 2:1–9.

Jeremiah: Never Too Young

> "Before I formed you in the womb I knew you. . . .
> I appointed you a prophet to the nations."

> (Jeremiah 1:5)

Jeremiah was marked and called by God even before his birth. At first Jeremiah was reluctant to take on the role of prophet. He pointed out to God that he was too young and did not have the skills to speak for God. God comforted Jeremiah by promising to go with Jeremiah and to speak through him. Jeremiah then received further instructions on how to face and denounce the tangle of evil all around him.

Like many young people today, Jeremiah felt inadequate for the great task God was asking him to carry out—he wasn't a good speaker, he was too young, and so on. God called Jeremiah to trust in God's power though, and God wants you to trust in God's power too.

How are young people today being called to change the world for the better?

Lord of youth and vigor, be my guide and mentor. Do not let me use my youth as an excuse for not speaking for you.

- To go deeper: Read Jeremiah 1:4–19.

Jeremiah: Rotten Underwear

> For as the loincloth clings to one's loins, so I made the whole of Israel and the whole house of Judah cling to me, says the LORD, in order that they might be for me a people. . . . But they would not listen.
>
> (Jeremiah 13:11)

God told Jeremiah to buy a new pair of underwear (a linen loincloth), wear it for a while, then take it off and hide it in the rocks along the Euphrates River. Days later the prophet was sent to dig up the loincloth. He found only a rotten, worthless rag. The new loincloth represented God's people when they were as close to God as underwear is to the body. But now the people had completely abandoned God and become like a rotten rag.

When we break our relationship with God, we too can feel as useless as dirty underwear. But remember that God is always waiting to cleanse us and re-establish our relationship.

When have you felt close to God? When have you felt like hiding under a rock?

God, are you really as close to me as underwear? Help me believe in your love.

- To go deeper: Read Jeremiah 13:1–11.

Jeremiah: Clay in God's Hands

> Just like the clay in the potter's hand, so are you in
> my hand, O house of Israel.
>
> (Jeremiah 18:5)

One day God invited Jeremiah to observe at the potter's
shop. The potter had the power to keep, destroy,
or reshape any of the vessels he made. The Lord told
Jeremiah that God was the potter and human beings the
clay. God could destroy those who chose evil, especially
those who were unjust and ignored the needs of the poor
and defenseless. But if God's people turned from their
evil ways, God would forgive them and build them up
again.

Each of us is clay in God's hands. God wants to shape
us and mold us into the beautiful vessels we were meant
to be—if we are but willing to allow God to work in our
lives. When we resist and refuse to live as God calls us to
live, we distort God's image in us.

When have you been open to letting God shape your
life? When have you resisted?

*Reshape me, potter God, so that I may be whole and
useful for your Reign.*

- To go deeper: Read Jeremiah 18:1–11.

Jeremiah: First Appearances Are Deceiving

> The LORD showed me [Jeremiah] two baskets of figs placed before the temple of the LORD.
>
> (Jeremiah 24:1)

About halfway through the Book of Jeremiah, the prophet is shown two baskets of beautiful ripe fruit, but he discovers that one basket of figs is actually rotten inside. The Lord told Jeremiah the good figs are like God's people who had been exiled because of their unfaithfulness but, having repented, would be built up and brought back. The bad fruits are like the remnant of Jerusalem, who would not change their ways and return to God with their whole heart.

Who is good and who is bad is not always obvious at first glance. We often judge others by outer appearances, but God looks at what is in our hearts.

When have you misjudged someone because of their outer appearance?

Lord of the good and the bad, you see into our hearts. Give me a heart that is true to you.

- To go deeper: Read Jeremiah 24:1–10.

Jeremiah: At the Bottom of a Well

So they took Jeremiah and threw him into the cistern,
. . . letting Jeremiah down by ropes.

(Jeremiah 38:6)

Throughout the years Jeremiah prophesied, he suffered humiliation, persecution, and imprisonment. But things looked really bad when he was lowered into a dark, muddy well to die. Then Ebedmelech, an Ethiopian, organized a rescue team to save him. Despite these many trials, Jeremiah continued to faithfully deliver God's message to the people of Jerusalem.

At times we feel we have fallen to the very bottom of life and can't get up. We are stuck in a situation that seems hopeless. We can get out only when God comes to our aid through people who love us and believe in us.

Have you ever felt like you have fallen into a dark well? Who helped you out?

Lord God, when things look dark and hopeless, help me remember you are always there to pull me out.

• To go deeper: Read Jeremiah 38:1–13.

Jeremiah: Led Astray

"My people have been lost sheep; their shepherds have led them astray.

(Jeremiah 50:6)

In speaking for God, Jeremiah often described the people of Jerusalem as "lost sheep," sheep who were in danger in the wilderness, sheep about to be destroyed by wild animals. Sheep follow their shepherd. So these animals were in danger when their shepherds were not acting responsibly. Jesus used this same comparison when speaking to his disciples.

Who are today's shepherds? One might say they are teachers, church leaders, politicians, and business leaders. They have a responsibility to lead people wisely and with compassion; we have a responsibility not to act like mindless sheep and follow them blindly.

Who are the shepherds today who lead people to live in a way that is pleasing to God?

God, you are the good shepherd. Help human shepherds like me lead people closer to you.

• To go deeper: Read Jeremiah 50:1–20.

Ezekiel: Prophet and Priest

> [The Lord] spread it before me; it had writing on the front and on the back, and written on it were words of lamentation and mourning and woe.
>
> (Ezekiel 2:10)

Ezekiel was among the eight thousand captives from Judah taken into exile in Babylon. God's people hoped the Exile would be brief, but their captivity lasted for seventy years. It was against this backdrop that Ezekiel, both priest and prophet, spoke God's words of hope. As prophet, Ezekiel was a powerful witness to God's truth and mighty deeds. As priest, Ezekiel gave structure to the community's life and worship.

Ezekiel was called by God to bring hope into a situation that was far from hopeful. We are sometimes called to be messengers of hope for others. Being an optimist is a wonderful gift.

When have you experienced a situation that seemed hopeless? Who brought you hope?

God, send me to those who need a ray of hope in their lives today.

- To go deeper: Read Ezekiel 2:1–10.

Ezekiel: Called to Speak

> Then I ate [the scroll], and in my mouth it was as sweet as honey.
>
> (Ezekiel 3:3)

Ezekiel was sent to the kingdom of Judah to speak God's sweet words of hope to the people so they would turn to God and avoid the siege of the Babylonians. God encouraged Ezekiel to preach God's word whether the people listened to him or not. We know they chose not to listen, and the Babylonian captivity ensued. Ezekiel then continued to prophesy during the Exile.

Because Ezekiel had experienced the sweetness of God's word, he could proclaim it with relentless conviction. God's word can become sweetness in our own lives when our faith is enlightened by the truth of God's word, and we are empowered to share our faith with others.

When has the word of God been like honey in your mouth?

God, your words are sweetness, for they are truth and light.

- To go deeper: Read Ezekiel 3:1–11.

Ezekiel: Heart of Flesh

> I will remove the heart of stone from their flesh and
> give them a heart of flesh.
>
> (Ezekiel 11:19)

Both Ezekiel and Jeremiah were concerned that God's people have hearts receptive to the word of God. When God's people have hearts of stone, they are stubborn and will not keep God's Commandments. However, when God's people have hearts of flesh, God's Law is no longer just words etched on stone tablets, but it is lived out with love in the actions of their everyday lives.

In the Mediterranean world, the heart is thought to be the center of a person's feelings and will. For us, the heart symbolizes love. When our hearts are healthy, they are filled with love for God and others. When our hearts are unhealthy, they become diseased; they turn rock hard and are unable to love.

When has your heart felt like a heart of flesh? Has it ever felt like a heart of stone?

God, give me a pure heart, a heart of flesh that desires to do your will.

- To go deeper: Read Ezekiel 11:14–21.

Ezekiel: The Good Shepherd

> You are my sheep, the sheep of my pasture and I
> am your God, says the Lord GOD.
>
> (Ezekiel 34:31)

According to Ezekiel, the kingdom of Judah was conquered by the Babylonians owing to poor leadership. Those who ruled made decisions based on their own self-interests rather than for the good of the whole community. Because their governance was oppressive and unjust, eventually the people no longer followed and, without good leaders, the whole kingdom perished.

Ezekiel presented God as the good shepherd who never abandoned or abused his flock. We have a right to have the same expectation of leadership today—that leaders in the Church and our civic communities will be like good shepherds, servant leaders who seek the common good of all over any personal gain.

When have you been a servant leader in your school, home, or community?

God, let me lead as you would lead, putting the good of others before any personal gain.

- To go deeper: Read Ezekiel 34:11–30.

Ezekiel: A Man of Visions

> The four had the faces of a human being, the face of a lion on the right side, the face of an ox on the left side, and the face of an eagle.
>
> (Ezekiel 1:10)

The significance of Ezekiel's vision of the living creatures with wings is that God's presence was mobile. Previously the Jewish people had believed God was present only in the Temple in Jerusalem. Now held captive far from Jerusalem and the Temple destroyed, the Jewish people felt that God was no longer present among them. Ezekiel's vision symbolized that God was present—even in Babylon—and that the Covenant with God continued.

The faces of the four creatures are the same symbols we use to represent the four Gospel writers (evangelists)—Matthew, Mark, Luke, and John. By using these four symbols, we acknowledge that God's presence and Covenant continue in our lives today.

How is God's presence evident today?

God, help me recognize your holy presence in my life.

• To go deeper: Read Ezekiel 1:1–28.

Ezekiel: Dry Bones

> I prophesied as [God] commanded me, and the
> breath came into them, and they lived, and stood
> on their feet, a vast multitude.
>
> (Ezekiel 37:10)

Ezekiel's vision of the dry bones' taking on flesh and coming to life offered hope to the Israelites at a time when hope seemed dead—hope that someday they would leave their captivity in Babylon and return to Jerusalem. Ezekiel prophesied that God would breathe new life into the Israelites, that God would once again restore the Temple and the kingdom of Judah.

In our faith life, we may experience times that seem like the dry bones in Ezekiel's vision. We may feel like our faith life is dead or that God is not present. Ezekiel reminds us that hope is found in the words of God. God's word renews our faith and breathes new life into our spirit.

When have you experienced dryness in your own faith life?

God, your word is the breath of life. Continue to move in me, renew and set aflame my faith.

• To go deeper: Read Ezekiel 37:1–14.

Ezekiel: The New Jerusalem

> Wherever the river goes, every living creature that swarms will live. . . . It will become fresh; and everything will live where the river goes.
>
> (Ezekiel 47:9)

Ezekiel's vision shows the extensive knowledge he had of the city of Jerusalem and of the Temple before its destruction. This vision preserved the hope of the Jewish people that there would someday be a new Jerusalem—one in which the river of God's hope would again flow and everything that came into contact with this water would be made new.

The waters of Baptism give us new life in Christ. We are made a new creation and become the light of Christ—hope—for our world. We are like life-giving water flowing from the Temple, refreshing and renewing everything that comes into contact with the water.

When have you been a source of renewed hope for another person?

God, make me a blessing for others, like the life-giving water in Ezekiel's vision.

- To go deeper: Read Ezekiel 47:1–12.

Daniel: A Holy Hero

> But Daniel resolved that he would not defile himself
> with the royal rations of food and wine.
>
> (Daniel 1:8)

Daniel was a legendary prophet of God—a holy hero—
who lived during one of the persecutions of the Israelites.
Courage, fidelity, and an ability to engender hope were
his hallmarks. Gifted with an athletic physique, good
looks, and wisdom, Daniel was chosen to serve in the
king's court. To show that his God would care for him,
Daniel consumed only vegetables and water. After ten
days of this diet, Daniel emerged healthier and stronger
than the other men in training who ate the royal rations.

Healthy eating, good nutrition, and dieting are common
concerns among young people today. Motivations range
from wanting to look good to wanting to run faster. Daniel's
concern, however, was a desire to rely on God.

What concerns do you have regarding food? How is
God a part of that concern?

*Guide me, Lord, as I seek to be nourished by your
presence in my life.*

- To go deeper: Read Daniel 1:1–21.

Daniel: The Writing on the Wall

"Give your rewards to someone else! Nevertheless, I will read the writing to the king and let him know the interpretation."

(Daniel 5:17)

When the pagan king desecrated the vessels that had been taken from the Temple in Jerusalem, he was confronted by a human hand writing on a plaster wall in the royal palace. Desperate to know the meaning of the message, the king sought out Daniel and promised to reward him if he could interpret it. Denying any desire for gifts, Daniel informed the king that because of the king's hardness of heart and pride, his kingdom would be divided and given to others.

When we are faced with our own faults and failings, we may be tempted to deny the reality before us. Denial, however, can keep us from reading the writing on the wall.

Who has helped you "read the writing on the wall" when your actions have been less than admirable?

Grant me, God, eyes to see and a heart to understand your "wall messages" to me.

• To go deeper: Read Daniel 5:1–30.

Daniel: Deliverance

> My God sent me his angel and shut the lions' mouths so that they would not hurt me, because I was found blameless before him.
>
> (Daniel 6:22)

As kings of the jungle, lions have always been viewed as symbols of death. Daniel's insistence on praying to God and not to the king resulted in his having to face death in the lions' den. Daniel courageously trusted in God and was rewarded by walking away unharmed. Not only was Daniel's life spared but also the king and the entire nation came to worship Daniel's God.

Sometimes being a teenager feels like being thrown into a lions' den. Having to confront classroom bullies, cliques, and friends turned foes can make a person feel like she or he is facing a ferocious lion or even death. As Daniel demonstrated, courage and trust in God are essential.

What situations have made you feel like you have been thrown into a lions' den?

Defender of those who trust you, and deliverer of all in danger, be with me in my hour of need.

• To go deeper: Read Daniel 6:1–28.

Daniel: Viewing the Vision

> As for me, Daniel, my spirit was troubled within me,
> and the visions of my head terrified me.
>
> (Daniel 7:15)

You awaken with a start and have a sinking feeling in your stomach—you have just had a nightmare. Daniel, the prophet of God, had just such an experience. His visions, which were rich in symbolic language but pointed to real people and real events, terrified him. Ultimately these visions pointed to the destruction of evil and the victory of God's Reign. Though Daniel admitted to being afraid of these visions, he was willing to reflect on them despite his fear.

Our dreams and visions of the future can be a source of fear and confusion for us as we try to decipher their meaning for our lives. Nevertheless, facing our fears is imperative to becoming all that God has called us to be.

What fears keep you from facing your dreams and visions?

Courage-giving God, guide me as I seek to face my fears and follow my dreams.

• To go deeper: Read Daniel 7:1–28.

Daniel: Seeking Answers

> Then I turned to the Lord God, to seek an answer by prayer and supplication with fasting and sackcloth and ashes.
>
> (Daniel 9:3)

Amid life's painful mysteries, our immediate response is simply to ask why? We want to make sense of what is happening and to find a reason for it. Daniel's response to Jerusalem's devastation was the same—he wanted an answer. How Daniel sought that answer is a model for all of us: he petitioned God's help for other people, proclaimed God's greatness, expressed sadness for wrongdoing, and asked for God's forgiveness.

Growing to adulthood can be difficult because of painful experiences that leave us looking for answers. When facing life's mysteries, we must turn to God with prayers of intercession, praise, sorrow, and petition.

When have the painful mysteries of life left you asking why?

Sustaining God, stay with me in times of suffering and pain. Guide me to you in prayer.

• To go deeper: Read Daniel 9:1–19.

Daniel: Saving Susanna

> God stirred up the holy spirit of a young lad named
> Daniel, and he shouted . . . "I want no part in
> shedding this woman's blood!"
>
> (Daniel 13:45–46)

Daniel came upon a woman who had been falsely
accused of making sexual propositions by two men who
desired to have sex with her. When she refused, they
claimed she had made advances toward them. She was
found guilty and sentenced to death. Daniel courageously
defended her innocence, and his bravery saved her life.

The scene is a familiar one. A crowd of friends has
gathered, and the conversation quickly turns to the latest
gossip about "friends" who are not present. No one's
blood is shed, but reputations are ruined and characters
are crushed by truths and untruths that are shared and
repeated. Displaying courage and speaking the truth can
be difficult when friends are speaking ill of one another.

Have you ever been stirred to speak up when friends
indulge in gossip?

*Spirit of courage, stir within me when I need to speak
your word of truth.*

• To go deeper: Read Daniel 13:1–64.

Daniel: Worshiping the Real

"Because I do not revere idols made with hands, but the living God, who created heaven and earth and has dominion over all living creatures."

(Daniel 14:5)

Researchers have often struggled to determine why people do what they do. The answer is elusive even when people seek to understand their own behavior. When people are asked to explain their behavior, a common response is, "I don't know." The prophet Daniel was not so indecisive. When the king commanded Daniel to give a reason for his not worshiping the idol Bel, Daniel did not hesitate to explain that he worshiped the living God—the Creator of heaven and earth.

Power, prestige, and pleasure are some of the idols people worship today. Like Daniel, we are called to worship the living God—the source of all power, prestige, and pleasure.

What reasons would you list for why you worship God?

God, may I always worship you and you alone in grateful praise.

- To go deeper: Read Daniel 14:1–22.

Ezra and Nehemiah: The Return to Jerusalem

> Thus says King Cyrus of Persia . . . any of those among you who are of [Yahweh's] people . . . are now permitted to go up to Jerusalem in Judah.
>
> (Ezra 1:2–3)

Ezra, a priest, and Nehemiah, the appointed governor of the area, returned to Jerusalem under the protective hand of the king of Persia after seventy years in Babylonian captivity. Together these two great men provided the leadership needed to rebuild Jerusalem, its Temple, and the city wall. Both are revered as great and holy men by Jewish people today.

Ezra and Nehemiah inspired the Jewish people to rebuild their lives in Jerusalem. They helped God's people to once again focus on living out God's Covenant. Through your example and leadership, you also have an opportunity to inspire others to renew their faith.

How do you inspire others to renew their faith and trust in God?

God, allow my faithfulness and trust in you to inspire others to renew their faith and trust in you.

- To go deeper: Read Ezra 1:1–11.

Ezra: Builder of the Second Temple

> When the builders laid the foundation of the temple of the LORD, the priests in their vestments were stationed to praise the LORD with trumpets, and the Levites, . . . with cymbals.
>
> (Ezra 3:10)

Upon his departure from Babylon, Ezra was given permission to collect funds from the Jews in Babylon and from the royal treasury in order to rebuild the Temple in Jerusalem. Rebuilding the Temple was a long and hard task that began in about 536 BC and was completed in 515 BC. As a scribe, Ezra continuously inspired the Jewish people to rebuild the Temple through regular teaching about the ways of Yahweh.

As a person of faith, you are given the same task as Ezra—to build up God's Church, the people of God. Therefore, whenever you build up or encourage others to live their faith, you are building up the Church of God.

How do you build up the Church, the people of God, each day?

God, give me the desire to build up your Church, and show me the many ways to do this.

- To go deeper: Read Ezra 3:8–13.

Ezra: God at the Center

> For Ezra had set his heart to study the law of the LORD, and to do it, and to teach the statutes and ordinances in Israel.
>
> (Ezra 7:10)

Ezra brought with him from Babylon a scroll of the Law. It was what remained of the Mosaic Law before the Babylonian captivity. It served as the norm for the Jewish faith and practices for many years. Thus Ezra has been credited not only with leading the rebuilding of the Temple but also with the restoration of the Mosaic Law, the way of living in accord with God's Covenant made with the Israelites at Mount Sinai.

The Law, or Torah as it is known today, is the center of the Jewish faith. It gives direction to all aspects of life for Jewish people. As Christians, the Gospels are the center of our faith. It is Jesus's teachings in the Gospels that direct our lives as disciples.

How do you allow the Gospels to serve as a guide for your life?

God, I seek to live my life according to your laws.

• To go deeper: Read Ezra 7:1–10.

Ezra: Sign of God's Favor

> Then we left the river Ahava on the twelfth day of the first month, to go to Jerusalem; the hand of our God was upon us.
>
> (Ezra 8:31)

The Edict of Cyrus in 538 BC initiated the restoration period that began with the Jewish people's returning from Babylon to Jerusalem. Upon reaching Jerusalem, the people found everything destroyed. Reconstruction of the city would be hard work that would take many years to complete. Under the leadership of Ezra, God's people embraced the task of rebuilding with hope-filled hearts because they knew God's favor was upon them.

Initially, many tasks in our life may seem overwhelming and unattainable. However, if we put forth our best effort and call upon God's blessings, little by little we will begin to see productive results.

What great things have you already accomplished because of your perseverance?

God, bless me with a spirit of perseverance so I may accomplish your will in my life.

- To go deeper: Read Ezra 8:31–36.

Nehemiah: A Man of Integrity

> In the month of Nisan, in the twentieth year of King Artaxerxes, when wine was served him, I carried the wine and gave it to the king.
>
> (Nehemiah 2:1)

Nehemiah served as a trusted servant of King Artaxerxes I in Persia's capital city of Susa. As the king's cup bearer, Nehemiah tested everything the king drank, making sure it had not been poisoned. Because of Nehemiah's faithful service, the king allowed him to return to Jerusalem so he could help God's people restore the city and the Temple.

Serving others faithfully is a way of serving God. Because Nehemiah was a man of integrity and people respected him, he was able to help his people. If we are people of integrity who live godly values, we will be able to speak credibly on behalf of others in need.

How have you been a person of integrity that has given faithful service to others?

God, may I always be a faithful servant of yours, caring for others as you care for me.

- To go deeper: Read Nehemiah 2:1–10.

Nehemiah: Governor of Judah

"You see the trouble we are in, how Jerusalem lies
in ruins with its gates burned. Come, let us rebuild
the wall of Jerusalem."

(Nehemiah 2:17)

Commissioned by the King of Persia as the governor of
the area, Nehemiah set about rebuilding the walls around
the city of Jerusalem. Nehemiah was undertaking an
immense task. Everything in Jerusalem was in utter chaos.
Despite the overwhelming situation, Nehemiah accepted
the challenge. The king helped Nehemiah by giving him
access to people who could provide needed building
materials and by sending members of the Persian army
to help.

When faced with the poverty and devastation Nehemiah faced, we might have been tempted to give up and
walk away rather than try to change the situation. Yet God
challenges us to stand up against injustice and to take
action.

How is God calling you to bring goodness out of
chaos?

*God, give me the strength to take action in difficult
and seemingly hopeless situations.*

- To go deeper: Read Nehemiah 2:11–20.

Nehemiah: Leader of Change

> So the wall was finished on the twenty-fifth day of
> the month of Elul, in fifty-two days.
>
> (Nehemiah 6:15)

It was under the direction of Nehemiah that the walls of
Jerusalem were rebuilt, and economic and social reforms
were enacted to restore order. Nehemiah's leadership was
essential as the Jewish people returned to Jerusalem and
rebuilt their lives. Along with economic and social reforms,
Nehemiah enacted religious reforms that eventually gave
rise to the beginning of modern Judaism.

Nehemiah's religious values and beliefs inspired others
to rebuild Jerusalem and brought about needed social
reforms. In the same way, basing our lives in the values of
the Gospel of Jesus Christ inspires others to do good. We
may not see immediate results, but if we are faithful, God
will bless our efforts.

How have you been a leader in helping others become
aware of social concerns?

*God, help me see the injustice in my world and be a
leader for change.*

- To go deeper: Read Nehemiah 12:27–43.

Job: Questioning Suffering

Job said . . . "Why did I not die at birth?"

(Job 3:2,11)

The Book of Job is a parable about a good man who suddenly had everything go wrong! The guy was happily married with a great family, wonderful flocks, bountiful lands, and plenty of money. Then in one day, his children, servants, and flocks were all killed. The mystery of why some people, even innocent people, have to suffer is questioned in chapter after chapter of Job, but we never do get an answer.

We continue to grapple with the mystery of suffering today as we try to make sense of the incomprehensible devastation and loss that people suffer. We are left asking God why. Why do so many people have to suffer and die because of terrorism, natural disasters, and war?

When have you experienced suffering that left you asking God why?

God, in the face of suffering, never let me lose hope or faith in you.

• To go deeper: Read Job 3:3–26.

Job: Tried and Tested

> The LORD said to Satan, "Very well, all that [Job] has
> is in your power."
>
> (Job 1:12)

The devil plays a lively role in the Book of Job. God was proud of his faithful and pious servant, Job. God bragged so much about Job that Satan couldn't stand it! Satan insisted that Job was faithful only because God had blessed him, and that if Job's possessions were taken away, he would turn from God. Confident in Job's faithfulness, God gave Satan the okay to do his best to turn Job away from God.

The Israelites believed that suffering was caused by sinfulness—either the sins of the person who suffered or because of the sins of that person's ancestors. In the story of Job, God uses Satan to show us that suffering is a part of the human condition and is not caused by sin.

When have you been tempted to blame someone's misfortune and suffering on sin in their life?

Dear God, help me be compassionate toward those who suffer, not judgmental of them.

- To go deeper: Read Job 1:1–22.

Job: Loyal and Faithful

> So Satan went out from the presence of the LORD,
> and inflicted loathsome sores on Job from the sole
> of his foot to the crown of his head.
>
> (Job 2:7)

Satan was still not convinced of Job's total loyalty to God
and was certain that if he made Job suffer bodily pain,
Job would give up and curse God. God permitted Satan
to inflict Job with boils, sores, and infected wounds on his
entire body. Job was barely recognizable to his wife and
friends. Job suffered and endured, refusing to curse God.

Despite his suffering, Job never lost faith in God. Even
though his friends and family encouraged him to blame
and curse God, Job suffered in silence and refused to
blame or complain.

The why of suffering is beyond explanation. How is it
possible to accept willingly what we cannot understand?

*God, why do you allow the young, the innocent, the
old, and the helpless to suffer? Help me hold on to
you, even though I do not understand.*

• To go deeper: Read Job 2:1–10.

Job: Comfort in Time of Need

> Now when Job's three friends heard of all these troubles that had come upon him, . . . they met together to go and console and comfort him.
>
> (Job 2:11)

Comforting a friend who is suffering is one of the finest acts of compassion you can perform. When Job's three friends found out Job was suffering, they went to comfort him. As they approached him, they hardly recognized him because of his pain, disease, and suffering. They cried out loud and tore their clothing in lament. Then in total unity with their suffering friend, they sat on the ground with him for seven days saying nothing.

Trying to console someone who is experiencing a great loss or a painful situation can be very difficult. We may not know what to say, and the pain of another can remind us of our own losses and mortality.

What keeps you from reaching out to console others?

Lord of loneliness and love, help me find the words, actions, and strength to console those who suffer.

- To go deeper: Read Job 2:11–13.

Job: Questioning God

"Therefore I [Job] will not restrain my mouth; I will speak in the anguish of my spirit. I will complain in the bitterness of my soul."

(Job 5:18)

Job moaned, complained, and questioned God; he scolded and fretted. He searched his past and present. Why was God doing this to him, an upright and pious man? Job's friends took turns questioning him and asked Job if he had committed some grave secret sin. Despite all the questions, Job continued to cling to his innocence. Throughout his ordeal, Job never stopped talking to God.

Job models for us how to handle suffering in our lives. Although we may not understand our suffering, we need to express our feelings to God—even if they are feelings of anger.

How do you cope in times of suffering? Have you ever been angry at God?

God, may I always be honest with you about how I feel and trust that you will see me through the painful times in life.

• To go deeper: Read Job 7:1–21.

Job: Beyond Understanding

"Hear this, O Job; stop and consider the wondrous works of God."

(Job 37:14)

Finally, after the long debate, God addressed Job's call for justice by asking some hard questions about creation and good and evil. The point of this final conversation between God and Job is that God is beyond all human understanding. Job and his friends could debate about God's actions all they wanted, but they would never be able to understand God fully because God's actions are more than the human mind can comprehend.

We can be so obsessed with trying to solve the mysteries of life that we miss the wonder of it all. Through Jesus's suffering on the cross, we can be sure the heart of God is never far from those who suffer. God's plan is beyond our understanding and, at best, we catch only a glimpse of it now and again.

How do the wonders of God's creation provide healing in your life?

Lord God, I stand in awe of the mystery of your healing presence in all of creation.

• To go deeper: Read Job 38:1—41:24.

Job: Accepting the Bad with the Good

> "I [Job] had heard of you [God] by the hearing of
> the ear, but now my eye sees you."
>
> (Job 42:5)

Suffering in the Book of Job is the art of accepting the bad with the good from God's hand. In the wonderful, almost fairy-tale, ending of the book, Job actually sees God. He has been talking to God day after day, and at long last in the closing chapters, he sees God. (He doesn't tell us what God looks like either!) This wonderful vision leaves Job stunned and humbled.

In the end, Job regained everything he had lost; in fact, he was given double what he had before. But Job's question about why he had to suffer is never completely answered. What Job's story does tell us is that even though there are no answers to suffering, God is near, suffers with us, and rewards patient suffering.

When has your suffering brought you closer to God?

Lord God, help me to pray like Job prayed and to know that you are near when I suffer.

• To go deeper: Read Job 42:7–17.

The Maccabees: Standing Alone

"I [Mattathias] and my sons and my brothers will continue to live by the covenant of our ancestors."

(1 Maccabees 2:20)

Mattathias, a devout and determined Jew, was the father and head of the Hasmonean family, who lived between 175 and 134 BC. Grounded in an allegiance to God that defied the pressures and persecutions of the Greeks, the Maccabees (as Mattathias's sons were called) came to exemplify unprecedented loyalty and dedication to God. They stood alone in their worship of God.

Standing alone is never easy, especially when you are trying to fit in and be accepted by others. When peer pressure pushes you to ignore your beliefs or betray your values, remembering the example of the Maccabees can be a source of courage.

Whom do you look to for support and inspiration in living out your beliefs and values?

Strengthen me, Lord, as I seek to live by your law of love, even if I must stand alone in my beliefs.

- To go deeper: Read 1 Maccabees 2:1–41.

The Maccabees: Words to the Wise

> Now, my children, show zeal for the law, and give your lives for the covenant of our ancestors.
>
> (1 Maccabees 2:50)

Deathbed discourses have a powerful impact on one's life. Mattathias knew he was dying, and he wanted to impart to his sons words of wisdom that would direct their lives after he was gone. Mattathias's greatest desire was that his sons be passionate in living what God required of them and be willing to give their lives for the Covenant that had been established between God and their ancestors.

It is not unusual for young people to be passionately involved in causes for social justice. They are often willing to give their all for what they believe in. This story in First Maccabees challenges us to ponder how passionate and zealous we are for God and the things of God.

How do you show your zeal for the law of God?

May your word ignite me with zeal for your law of love, Lord.

- To go deeper: Read 1 Maccabees 2:49–69.

The Maccabees: Daring Dedication

> So they celebrated the dedication of the altar for eight days, and joyfully offered burnt offerings; they offered a sacrifice of well-being and a thanksgiving offering.
>
> (1 Maccabees 4:56)

After Judas Maccabeus and his brothers took back the Temple from their enemies, they restored the Temple and reclaimed it for worship. They tore down the altar that had been profaned and built a new one, rebuilt the interior of the Temple, and crafted new vessels for worship. Then the Jewish people celebrated the dedication of the altar for eight days and gave thanks to God that their faith had survived.

It takes dedication, hard work, and discipline to master the arts and succeed in sports. But just as important as these things is celebrating our accomplishments by taking time to thank God.

When have you been dedicated to accomplishing something difficult?

Lord, may I always give you thanks for what you have accomplished through me.

- To go deeper: Read 1 Maccabees 4:36–60.

The Maccabees: Called to Lead

> "Now therefore we have chosen you today to take his place as our ruler and leader, to fight our battle."
>
> (1 Maccabees 9:30)

Judas Maccabeus had successfully led his people against persecuting armies and had even reclaimed the Temple in Jerusalem. But in the end, many of his men fled in fear of the Greek Syrian army, and Judas and his loyal followers were killed. Desperate for someone to lead them, the Israelites turned to Judas's brother Jonathan, who accepted the leadership of his people.

High school is often when young people first experience taking on a leadership role. School responsibilities or extracurricular activities provide an arena for trying out leadership skills. Although being a leader may not be as dramatic as it was during the time of the Maccabees, it still provides an opportunity to use the gifts God has given us.

In what ways are you called to lead others?

Lord and leader of all your people, show me the way to lead others to you.

- To go deeper: Read 1 Maccabees 9:23–31.

Eleazar: Teaching by Example

"By bravely giving up my life now, I will show myself worthy of my old age and leave to the young a noble example."

(2 Maccabees 6:27–28)

Eleazar (a respected, elderly scribe who lived during the time of the Maccabees) was well aware of the power of setting an example. Pressured by friends to pretend he was partaking of the forbidden meat, he refused. Preferring to remain true to his principles, Eleazar courageously embraced death by torture. Eleazar realized that the advantage of living a brief moment longer couldn't be compared to providing an example of nobility and courage for the young.

As we journey through life, each of us is called to be an example of goodness for younger generations while at the same time looking for examples of goodness in previous generations.

Who are the "elders" who have been an example of goodness for you?

God of all courage, grant me strength to live as Christ did, to be an example for others.

- To go deeper: Read 2 Maccabees 6:18–31.

The Maccabees: A Family of Courage

> It happened also that seven brothers and their mother were arrested and were being compelled by the king, under torture . . . to partake of unlawful swine's flesh.
>
> (2 Maccabees 7:1)

Torture as a means to influence others has been employed through the centuries. The story of the seven brothers and their mother in Second Maccabees is a classic example of courage amid horrendous cruelty. One by one, all of them were tortured in order to get them to deny their faith. As they witnessed one another's cruel death, the brothers and their mother encouraged and supported one another with words of hope and comfort.

It is difficult to imagine having to experience such cruelty. Unfortunately, torture is still used by extremists today as a means of persecuting individuals for their beliefs.

What beliefs would you be willing to give your life for?

Deepen my desire, Lord, not only to live for you but to be willing to give my life for you.

• To go deeper: Read 2 Maccabees 7:1–42.

The Maccabees: Remembering the Dead

> For if he were not expecting that those who had fallen would rise again, it would have been superfluous and foolish to pray for the dead.
>
> (2 Maccabees 12:44)

Reverence for the dead has existed since ancient times. As leader of the Israelite army, Judas Maccabeus offered prayers for those who had fallen in battle. His belief in life after death was compelling. Realizing that some of his fallen soldiers had turned from God, Judas offered prayers and atonement for the sins of his men, confident that they would be forgiven and enjoy eternal reward.

Death touches all our lives as loved ones, neighbors, and friends complete their journeys here on earth. Praying for those who have died keeps us united to our loved ones and attests to our belief in resurrection.

What is your prayer for your loved ones who have died?

Lord of life, keep me close to my loved ones who have gone before me in death.

- To go deeper: Read 2 Maccabees 12:38–45.

Joseph: Faith in Action

Joseph [was] the husband of Mary, of whom Jesus was born, who is called the Messiah.

(Matthew 1:16)

We know very little of Joseph from the Scriptures. What is known can be found in the Gospels of Matthew and Luke. We are introduced to Joseph as the man to whom Mary is engaged. He is described as a righteous person who listens to God and allows God to lead him. The last time Joseph is mentioned in the Scriptures is when Jesus, at the age of twelve, is left behind in Jerusalem after Passover. After three days of searching for him, Joseph and Mary find Jesus in the Temple. Joseph never speaks in any of the Gospel accounts.

There is strength in silence. Joseph's words may not have been recorded, but his love and devotion for God and his family speak louder than any words could. Joseph modeled faith in action.

Are you, like Joseph, a person who speaks through actions?

God, let me always be aware of the power of my actions.

• To go deeper: Read Matthew 1:18–25.

Joseph: Exemplary Husband

> The angel Gabriel was sent by God to a town in Galilee called Nazareth, to a virgin [Mary] engaged to a man whose name was Joseph, of the house of David.
>
> (Luke 1:26–27)

God chose Joseph to play a significant role in salvation history, that of husband to Mary and foster father to Jesus. It is within this community of love between Joseph and Mary that God placed his beloved Son. An exemplary husband and father, Joseph provided his family with love, protection, and sustenance. The image of Joseph painted in the Scriptures is one of a person filled with the grace of God.

God had placed on Joseph a huge responsibility—one that many men would have run from. But Joseph trusted God completely and lived out his vocation as Mary's husband and the father of God's Son as best as he could.

What vocation—married life, single life, religious life, priesthood—is God calling you to?

God, help me discover what vocation you are calling me to and give me the grace to live it.

• To go deeper: Read Luke 1:26–38.

Joseph: Descendant of King David

> An account of the genealogy of Jesus the Messiah, the son of David, the son of Abraham . . . and Jacob the father of Joseph the husband of Mary, of whom Jesus was born.
>
> (Matthew 1:1)

During the time of Joseph, family lineage was traced exclusively through the father. Joseph's ancestral line provided an uninterrupted link to David and, even further back, to Abraham. The belief that the Messiah would be a descendant of David was based on the prophet Nathan's promise to David (see 2 Samuel 7:16). It is noteworthy that the final link in Matthew's account of Jesus's genealogy was a woman—Mary, the wife of Joseph.

Genealogy has newfound interest today as many people seek to trace their family roots in hopes of learning more about themselves. Knowing whom and where we have come from is important in understanding who we are and what God is calling us to.

What about your own heritage are you most proud of?

God, thank you for the blessing of my ancestors.

• To go deeper: Read Matthew 1:1–17.

Joseph: Righteous Man

> [Mary's] husband Joseph, being a righteous man and unwilling to expose her to public disgrace, planned to dismiss her quietly.
>
> (Matthew 1:19)

The Gospel of Matthew tells us that Joseph was a righteous man who knew God's Law and lived his life in accordance with those precepts. Because Joseph had a deep sense of what was just and right, he chose to deal with Mary, who was pregnant with a child that was not his, in the most kind and humane way possible at that time. After a lot of prayer and reflection, Joseph decided to send Mary away quietly rather than expose her to public ridicule.

Righteousness is a virtue that all Christians are called to live. To know what is right and just, we first have to come to know and understand the way of God's love. Then we need to apply this wisdom to all we do.

Whom do you consider to be righteous? How are you becoming more loving and just?

God, make me strong and loving as I learn how to be a righteous person like Joseph.

• To go deeper: Read Matthew 1:18–19.

Joseph: Good Father

[Joseph] went to be registered with Mary, to whom he was engaged and who was expecting a child. While they were [in Bethlehem], the time came for her to deliver her child.

(Luke 2:5–6)

In the events surrounding Jesus's birth, Joseph recognized God's active presence in Jesus's life. He witnessed the shepherds who, because of a vision of angels, came to reveal that Jesus was the Messiah. As a devout Jew, Joseph was present and active in all that was required upon the birth of a firstborn son according to the Law of Moses—from naming the child to presenting the child in the Temple. A good father, Joseph recognized how special Jesus was and guided his growth in faith.

Fathers and father figures play an important role in our lives, especially as we grow and develop. They can help us discover who we are and remind us whose we are.

What qualities make a good father?

God, thank you for your fatherly presence in all stages of growth in my life.

• To go deeper: Read Luke 2:1–20.

Joseph: Protector of Life

> Then Joseph got up, took the child and his mother by night, and went to Egypt.
>
> (Matthew 2:14)

In a dream, God revealed to Joseph the danger that threatened his family and directed Joseph to take the child and Mary to safety. Joseph did not hesitate to protect his family and immediately took them to Egypt. Because Joseph had a deep relationship with God, he trusted God's word to him. At the same time, it must have been difficult to live as exiles in a foreign country. Having fled persecution, Joseph now had to fend for his family amid a strange culture and people.

To be a protector of life is not exclusively the role of a father; it should be the number one priority for each of us. Many forces run counter to the preservation of life, so we must work diligently to protect life at all stages.

How do you protect the gift of life through your actions, speech, and attitudes?

God of life, like Joseph, may I always be a protector of life.

- To go deeper: Read Matthew 2:13–18.

Joseph: Provider

> There [Joseph] made his home in a town called Nazareth.
>
> (Matthew 2:23)

Upon hearing that it was safe to return to the land of Israel, Joseph moved his family to Nazareth. It was in this small town in the Galilee area that Joseph provided for his family as a carpenter. His family relied upon Joseph's skilled hands to gain an income to sustain them. Joseph understood the feeling of accomplishment gained through the quality woodworking he was engaged in and, as was custom, mentored his son in the family business.

Families and communities today continue to rely on the skills of its members for support. When planning a career, it is important to consider not only the skills and training that are necessary but also how that job serves the wider community.

What type of occupation or career would you like to pursue?

God, as I look to my future with excitement, please guide my decisions so that my life's work will be of service to my family and others.

• To go deeper: Read Matthew 2:19–23.

Mary of Nazareth: First Disciple

The angel said to her, "Do not be afraid, Mary."

(Luke 1:30)

Mary, a young Jewish girl of fifteen or sixteen years old, was engaged to marry Joseph when an extraordinary visit by an angel changed her life. The angel announced that Mary had been chosen to be the mother of the promised Messiah. Mary was perplexed and afraid at first. She didn't understand how God could work such wonders in her life, because she was not yet married. Despite her fears, Mary said yes to doing God's will and became the first disciple to follow Jesus.

Being unwed and pregnant in Mary's time and culture had serious consequences, possibly even death. No wonder Mary was afraid. Yet Mary didn't let her fears keep her from doing what God asked of her. She took comfort in the knowledge that God was with her.

What fears keep you from doing what God asks of you?

Mary, your yes allowed God to become human. Mother of Jesus, pray for me.

• To go deeper: Read Luke 1:26–38.

Mary of Nazareth: Bearer of Good News

> Mary set out and went with haste to a Judean town in the hill country, where she entered the house of Zechariah and greeted Elizabeth.
>
> (Luke 1:39)

After Mary had been asked to be the mother of Jesus, the angel told Mary that her elderly relative Elizabeth, who had not been able to have children, was now six months pregnant. Already with child herself, Mary set out at once to visit and help Elizabeth prepare for the birth of her son. As the two women greeted each other joyfully, Elizabeth felt the child within her jump for joy and at that moment knew that Mary was the one who would give birth to the Messiah.

Mary's generosity and youthful energy were great gifts she offered without concern for herself. She continually put the needs of others before her own. Mary carried the Good News to others by the way she lived.

How do your actions bring the Good News of Jesus Christ to others?

Mary, you placed concern for others above your own needs. Help me be as generous.

- To go deeper: Read Luke 1:36–56.

Mary of Nazareth: Queen of Heaven

A great [sign] appeared in heaven: a woman clothed with the sun. . . . She was pregnant and was crying out in birth pangs.

(Revelation 12:1–2)

This vision taken from the Book of Revelation tells of a great battle between the forces of good and evil. The woman symbolically represents both Mary and the Church, who are about to give birth to the child who will conquer all evil, Jesus Christ.

This passage is read during the feast of the Assumption of Mary, when the Church celebrates Mary's faithfulness to the mission of Jesus and her entrance into the heavenly kingdom. The Church teaches that Mary was so honored and beloved by God that Mary did not die, but simply fell asleep and her body was taken to heaven. Mary's participation in her Son's Resurrection anticipates our own deliverance from death.

How has Mary taught you to be a servant of God's Reign?

Queen of heaven, teach me to be as faithful to God's plan as you were.

• To go deeper: Read Revelation 12:1–6.

Mary of Nazareth: Pondering the Good News

> But Mary treasured all these words and pondered them in her heart.
>
> (Luke 2:19)

The days leading up to the birth of her son were not easy ones for Mary. She and Joseph had to make a difficult journey to Bethlehem to participate in a census. Then when they finally arrived in the city, Mary went into labor and gave birth in a stable. It was the poor shepherds who would be the first to recognize and proclaim that this child, born to a woman from Nazareth, was really God's Son.

Perhaps what Mary reflected on when she heard the shepherds' words were the many contradictions in her life. Mary was a virgin, yet she was pregnant. She was lying in a stable, yet giving birth to a king. Her Son had power over life and death, yet it was the poor and the powerless who recognized him.

When have you been surprised by God working through the unexpected?

God, may I always wonder and reflect on the unexpected ways you enter my life.

- To go deeper: Read Luke 2:1–20.

Mary of Nazareth: Model for the Church

[Jesus's] mother said to the servants, "Do whatever he tells you."

(John 2:5)

Mary, Jesus, and the disciples were at a wedding in Cana when the wine suddenly ran out in the middle of the celebration. Mary, attentive to how this would reflect on the young couple and their families, immediately went to Jesus and told him of the situation, confident that he would help. Despite Jesus's protest that it was not his time, Mary went to the servants and instructed them to follow what Jesus tells them.

Like Mary, we are to be attentive and compassionate to the needs of those around us, to intercede for others before God, to have confidence that God will answer our prayers, to point to Jesus as the source of life, and to encourage others to follow Jesus's words.

Who is in need of your prayers? Whom are you called to lead to Christ?

God, help me remember to pray for the needs of others today.

- To go deeper: Read John 2:1–12.

Mary of Nazareth: Sorrowful Mother

> Then Simeon blessed them and said to [Jesus's] mother Mary, . . . "and a sword will pierce your own soul too."
>
> (Luke 2:34–35)

One can only imagine the sorrow Mary experienced as she witnessed her son's life and death unfold before her. She must have been frantic when she discovered that Jesus, only twelve years old, had been left behind in Jerusalem. She must have worried about Jesus's every move as he preached his message across the countryside, knowing that powerful religious and political leaders were out to trap and destroy her son. Then the sorrow beyond all sorrows, she must have been pushed to the point of despair when she watched her son being ridiculed, tortured, and executed.

Mary watched and wept but never gave up hope. She clung to the knowledge that someday her sorrow would be turned into immense joy.

Have you watched someone you love suffer? How overwhelming were your feelings?

Mary, help us cling to hope in sorrowful times.

• To go deeper: Read Luke 2:22–35.

Mary of Nazareth: Mother of the Church

> And from that hour the disciple took [Mary] into his own home.
>
> (John 19:27)

It was at the foot of the cross, before Jesus breathed his last breath, that he entrusted the care of Mary to his beloved disciple. From that point on, Mary would now forever be known as mother of the Church. Mary's yes gave birth to the foundation stone upon which the Church was built. Mary's faithfulness in fulfilling her role in salvation history forever gives new life and love to the Church.

As our mother, Mary is someone we can turn to when we are in need of guidance, counsel, inspiration, courage, patience, and solace. She accompanied Jesus on his journey through life, and now she walks with us.

Who builds up the life of your parish? How are you being called to contribute to the life of your parish?

Mary, mother of the Church, more than ever our Church needs you. Help me be a responsible member of my parish.

- To go deeper: Read John 19:25–30.

Elizabeth and Zechariah: Childless

> But [Elizabeth and Zechariah] had no children, because Elizabeth was barren, and both were getting on in years.
>
> (Luke 1:7)

Zechariah, a priest, and Elizabeth, from the tribe of Aaron, were a God-fearing couple who longed for a child to crown their marriage. Now that they both were getting older, it appeared they would never fulfill their dream. For a married couple in the ancient world, being childless was a tremendous disgrace. Zechariah and Elizabeth had a duty to become a family. The Jews knew from their history of persecution and exile that their race would survive only if there were descendants.

Even though having children is seen differently today, children are still considered a blessing by most people. All children bring unique gifts to their family and would be sadly missed if something ever happened to them.

What gifts do you bring to your family?

Lord of all, thank you for my parents and their willingness to give me life.

• To go deeper: Read Luke 1:5–7.

Elizabeth and Zechariah: Preparing for Greatness

> Your wife Elizabeth will bear you a son, and . . . he will be great in the sight of the Lord.
>
> (Luke 1:13–14)

Zechariah was startled when an angel appeared to him and told him he and his wife, Elizabeth, would soon give birth to a son who was destined to do great things. Zechariah and Elizabeth were instructed by the angel to raise the boy carefully. They were to make sure the child lived a holy life, for he would be a great prophet who would prepare God's people for the Messiah.

It is not uncommon for parents to invest large amounts of time and money in their children's education with the hopes of nurturing their full potential. God has destined each of us for great things and wants us to nurture that potential by living a holy life.

What potential do your parents see in you? How are you living a holy life?

Lord, help me to live a holy life and to remember that you have a great purpose for me.

- To go deeper: Read Luke 1:8–16.

Zechariah: Waiting in Silence

Because you [Zechariah] did not believe my words
. . . you will become mute, unable to speak, until
the day these things occur.

(Luke 1:20)

Zechariah was forced to wait in silence for the birth of his son. He doubted the angel's words, believing Elizabeth was too old to have a child. He didn't think it possible that God could perform such a miracle. Yet nothing is impossible for God! Soon after the angel spoke to Zechariah, new life began to grow within his wife, Elizabeth.

Zechariah had prayed to God for a son, but when the angel told him God had answered his prayer, he didn't believe. Often we pray for things but doubt that God can really answer our prayers. Like Zechariah, we need to become silent so we can hear God's answer and believe.

When have you prayed for something but doubted God could answer your prayer?

God, help me believe all things are possible for those who love you.

• To go deeper: Read Luke 1:18–25.

Elizabeth: Radiating God's Presence

Elizabeth was filled with the Holy Spirit.

(Luke 1:42)

As Elizabeth's weight of pregnancy grew heavier, her days were brightened by the visit of her young relative, Mary of Nazareth. Mary arrived excited and in transparent joy, for she too had new life within her. When the women first greeted each other, Elizabeth felt the infant in her womb leap for joy. At that moment, God's Spirit came upon Elizabeth and together she and Mary praised God for the message of the angel—God's Word—which was taking flesh.

Elizabeth felt God's presence as soon as she heard the sound of Mary's voice. Some individuals seem to radiate God's presence in their lives. Mother Teresa was one of those persons who could light up a room with God's presence. Her love for God was infectious and attracted many followers.

Whom do you know that radiates God's presence? How do you let God's presence shine in your life?

God, let the light of my faith shine for all to see so others will want to follow you.

• To go deeper: Read Luke 1:39–56.

Elizabeth and Zechariah: Seeing and Believing

[Zechariah] asked for a writing tablet and wrote, "His name is John."

(Luke 1:63)

The gift of a child to Elizabeth and Zechariah was cause for great rejoicing all over town! The child was, as promised by the angel, a fine healthy boy, and neighbors were sure the parents would name him after his father, Zechariah. So when Elizabeth insisted the child was to be named John, friends and relatives were astounded. Zechariah, still mute for doubting the angel, confirmed it by writing the name John on a tablet. Immediately Zechariah was able to speak.

Until Zechariah witnessed the birth of his son, he had refused to believe God's promise to him. He had to see with his own eyes before he stopped doubting. Sometimes, like Zechariah, we want to see before we believe God can bring new life into our lives.

When have you doubted God's promise of salvation to you?

Merciful God, may I believe in your saving grace even when it seems impossible.

• To go deeper: Read Luke 1:57–66.

Zechariah: Prayer of Praise

> Then [the child's] father Zechariah was filled with
> the Holy Spirit and spoke this prophecy.
>
> (Luke 1:67)

At the birth of his son, Zechariah was filled with God's
Spirit and began to praise God. This prayer, often called
the *Benedictus* (Latin for "blessed"), is a companion
piece to Mary's earlier prayer in Luke, the *Magnificat*.
It acknowledges and praises God's care and saving
power throughout Israel's history. Zechariah connects all
these wonders with the wonders of his newborn son and
the role John will have in preparing God's people for the
Messiah.

The prayers of Zechariah and Mary have become part
of the Church's official daily prayer called the Liturgy of
the Hours. The Church prays these prayers as part of the
beginning and end of each day as a way to acknowledge
that each of our lives, from dawn until dusk, is a part of
salvation history.

What great things has God done in your life?

*Write your own prayer of praise thanking God for the
gifts you have been blessed with.*

• To go deeper: Read Luke 1:67–80.

Elizabeth and Zechariah: Examples of Faith

"What then will this child become?"

(Luke 1:66)

Zechariah and Elizabeth must have wondered, along with their neighbors, how God's plan of salvation would unfold in their son's life. It was the example Zechariah and Elizabeth set in their own lives that prepared their son for his mission. Zechariah's life of service, offering prayers and sacrifices on behalf of God's people, prepared John for the rigid life of self-sacrifice he would need to live in order to credibly proclaim repentance. Elizabeth's complete trust in God's word prepared John to speak the truth in the face of persecution.

"Actions speak louder than words" is an old proverb that rings true when we talk about passing on faith from one generation to the next. The people who demonstrate their faith by their actions show us how faith is real today.

Who is a lived example of faith for you?

God, bless those who help educate me in the faith.

• To go deeper: Read Mark 1:1–8.

John the Baptist: The Last Great Prophet

> And you, child, will be called the prophet of the Most High; for you will go before the Lord to prepare his ways.
>
> (Luke 1:76)

John was the last of the great prophets God sent to the Israelites to prepare them for the coming of the Messiah. The son of aging parents, Zechariah and Elizabeth, John had been given a significant role in salvation history. He was chosen by God before his birth to be the one to stand at the threshold between the old and the new and point people to Jesus. John holds an honored position in the Church, serving as God's voice in proclaiming the Good News that the Messiah has come.

We also have a significant role in salvation history. In Baptism each of us has been called to proclaim the Good News and to lead others to Christ through the example of our lives.

How do you continue John's legacy of leading others to Jesus?

God, you need voices today to proclaim what Jesus taught. Allow me to be a humble voice.

- To go deeper: Read Luke 1:67–80.

John the Baptist: Encounter with God

> When Elizabeth heard Mary's greeting, the child leaped in her womb.
>
> (Luke 1:41)

When Mary, who was pregnant with Jesus, visited her cousin Elizabeth, the child within Elizabeth moved. While still in his mother's womb, John became aware of the presence of God and, in essence, leaped for joy. God's presence in John's life grew only deeper throughout his life.

We long to be stirred with the awareness of God's presence in our own lives—to be moved to joy. Often, though, when we do sense God's presence, we allow other things in our lives to distract us. Being aware of God's presence takes a commitment to focusing on what is truly important.

When have you leaped for joy because you knew you had encountered God?

God, keep me open to the many and varied ways you make your presence known in my life.

- To go deeper: Read Luke 1:39–45.

John the Baptist: Witness to Truth

> But the angel said to him, "Do not be afraid, Zechariah, for your prayer has been heard. Your wife Elizabeth will bear you a son, and you will name him John."
>
> (Luke 1:13)

While in the Temple sanctuary, an angel appeared to Zechariah and announced that God had heard his request and would give him a son. This child would have the spirit and power of Elijah (the greatest prophet until now). He would convert hearts and bring people to righteousness and wisdom. God chose John to make ready the way of the Lord—the Messiah.

On August 29, the Catholic Church celebrates the feast of the death of John the Baptist. The Church reveres John because he served as a witness to the truth, even in the face of arrest and execution. The Church today continues to need those willing to risk their lives as witnesses to the truth.

What risks do you take to witness to the truth of the Gospel?

God, help me live a life that imitates John's unceasing witness to your truth.

- To go deeper: Read Luke 1:5–25.

John the Baptist: Herald of Jesus

"I am the voice of one crying out in the wilderness,
'Make straight the way of the Lord.'"

(John 1:23)

After spending time in the desert praying and fasting, John came to understand he was the one chosen to prepare others for the coming of the Messiah. The words of Isaiah, "Make straight the way of the Lord," became John's mission statement. Fearlessly and boldly, John went about preaching and baptizing, knowing he was ushering in God's Reign. When Jesus arrived to begin his public ministry, John knew it was time to step aside.

It is not easy to take on a big project or to start some initiative and then have to hand it over to someone else. John's response was to humbly step aside because he knew his work pointed to a greater work that would be accomplished in Jesus Christ.

How comfortable are you in stepping aside so others can complete a work you began?

God, help me direct others you and to humbly know when my work is finished.

• To go deeper: Read John 1:19–34.

John the Baptist: Mission of Justice

> Whoever has two coats must share with anyone who has none; and whoever has food must do likewise.
>
> (Luke 3:11)

John and Jesus had a parallel mission that was grounded in social justice. In the tradition of all the great prophets, these two men preached, with conviction, a message of reconciliation that challenged the world to be more just. The sharp edge of the message of social justice is that it makes listeners uncomfortable because they realize they must make changes in their lives to correct the injustice.

Unfair distribution of food, shelter, and clothing is still a social justice issue today. It is easy to become complacent, thinking the issue is too big for one person to change. The message of the Gospel is that we can never be complacent whenever there is injustice.

How do you work to bring about justice in your community?

God, give me the eyes to see injustice, the courage to confront it, and the zeal to eliminate it.

• To go deeper: Read Luke 3:1–20.

John the Baptist: Appearance of a Prophet

Now John was clothed with camel's hair, with a leather belt around his waist, and he ate locusts and wild honey.

(Mark 1:6)

John dressed as a prophet. The cloak of camel's hair was a sign of a prophet. His garment was tied at his waist with a leather belt. John called God's people to turn from sin toward the good news of God's saving love. To the people of John's day, there was no mistaking him for anything but a prophet. Some even thought John was the great prophet Elijah, who had been taken up into heaven in a fiery chariot and now returned.

John was easily identified as a prophet by the people he lived and preached among, but prophets are not so easy to recognize today. We don't have a prophet uniform or clothing style. But if you hear someone taking a public and courageous stance against injustice, he or she is acting as a prophet.

Who speaks the message of God's justice today?

God, help me discern your prophets in my world today.

• To go deeper: Read Mark 1:1–8.

John the Baptist: Arrest and Execution

For Herod himself had sent men who arrested John, bound him, and put him in prison.

(Mark 6:17)

John was imprisoned by Herod Antipas, the son of Herod the Great. John had provoked his anger by accusing Herod of breaking Jewish Law in marrying his half brother's wife, Herodias. On the birthday of Herod, Herodias's daughter danced for the king and his guests. The dance pleased the king so much that he granted her anything she requested. After quickly consulting with her mother, she returned with the request of John the Baptist's head. The king fulfilled his promise and had John beheaded.

John was put to death because he challenged the corrupt ways of the royal family that ruled Galilee. Corruption still exists today, and truth is seen as the enemy that exposes it for what it is.

Who is a voice of truth against corruption today?

God, give me the gift of fortitude in facing corruption and evil in the world.

• To go deeper: Read Mark 6:14–29.

Jesus of Nazareth: No Perfect Family

> So all the generations from Abraham to David are
> fourteen generations . . . to the Messiah, fourteen
> generations.
>
> (Matthew 1:17)

It is not unusual for young people to become frustrated
with the rules and regulations of an older generation or to
point out the faults and failings of their parents and other
family members. An old Chinese proverb reminds us, "No
family can hang out the sign, 'Nothing the matter here!'"

Matthew's Gospel places the Son of God amid a
very human ancestry that spanned many generations
and included schemers, deceivers, adulterers, and even
murderers. Our Lord, being both human and divine, was
not ashamed of being related to an ancestry that knew
sin. In fact, it was for such as these that he was born,
lived, died, and rose.

Which members of your family do you sometimes
have difficulty acknowledging?

*God, may I always be grateful for those who have
given me life and those who have sustained it.*

- To go deeper: Read Matthew 1:1–17.

Jesus of Nazareth: A Stable Beginning

> And [Mary] gave birth to her firstborn son and wrapped him in bands of cloth, and laid him in a manger.
>
> (Luke 2:7)

Jesus's desire to nourish us is attested to by the setting in which his life began. We know from the Gospel and from tradition that Jesus was born in a manger, a feeding trough for animals, in the small town of Bethlehem, which means "house of bread." Jesus fulfills our needs, even our most basic need—hunger—by literally becoming bread to be shared by all.

We often rely on possessions as a means to finding fulfillment in life. Jesus's humble beginnings and reliance upon others tells us it is our connection with God and others, not what we have, that brings us fulfillment in life.

In what ways have you discovered God's nourishing presence in your life?

Babe of Bethlehem, teach me that life is nourished by your presence and not by many possessions.

• To go deeper: Read Luke 2:1–20.

Jesus of Nazareth: Temple Trauma

> [Jesus] went down with them and came to Nazareth, and was obedient to them.
>
> (Luke 2:51)

The only story of Jesus as a young person is found in Luke's Gospel and takes place during the Passover festival in Jerusalem. It is the story of Jesus's wandering off from Mary and Joseph at the age of twelve and his parents' search for him, ending with Jesus's returning to Nazareth with his parents, remaining obedient to them.

Like Jesus's who was celebrating with his parents, most young people can point to times of happiness and joy with their families. At other times, young people, like Jesus, wander off or do things that cause their parents to worry and question their behavior. In the end, however, Jesus's final response of obedience is crucial. We also are called to loving obedience.

When have you celebrated with your family? When have you caused them to worry?

Teach me, Lord, to celebrate with my family and to always return with a listening heart when I wander away from them.

• To go deeper: Read Luke 2:41–52.

Jesus of Nazareth: Recognized and Empowered

> And a voice came from heaven, "You are my Son, the Beloved; with you I am well pleased."
>
> (Mark 1:11)

We can only imagine how the words of his Father touched Jesus as he came out of the waters of his baptism. Jesus's public baptism points to his desire to be one with his Father and the Holy Spirit but also to his desire to be one with God's people. After his forty days in the wilderness, Jesus's ministry was about to begin.

Like Jesus, we not only acknowledge our oneness with God but also our commitment to serve others through the celebration of the sacrament of Confirmation. Recognizing we are God's beloved, we are empowered, like Jesus was, to go forth to serve God's people.

When has being loved empowered you to serve?

Loving Lord, open my heart so that I may recognize your words of love.

- To go deeper: Read Mark 1:9–11.

Jesus of Nazareth: The Feast Continues

> And Jesus said to [his mother], "Woman, what concern is that to you and to me? My hour has not yet come."
>
> (John 2:4)

In the story of the wedding at Cana, Jesus faced the sensitive request of his mother, whose compassionate heart saw the dilemma of the hosts who had run short on wedding wine. Jesus initially appeared to hesitate. Mary, not deterred by Jesus's statement, set the stage for Jesus to begin his public ministry by telling the servants, "Do whatever he tells you." After instructing the servants to fill the jugs with water, Jesus provided for the wedding guests the best of wines—the feast continued!

Note that Jesus did not begin his ministry alone but with the help of others. We also are called to work with others as we continue the mission of Jesus.

Whom do you work with in continuing the mission of Jesus? How does this encourage you?

Jesus, help me recognize where you are calling me to serve.

- To go deeper: Read John 2:1–12.

Jesus of Nazareth: Ultimate Teacher

> So if I, your Lord and Teacher, have washed your feet, you also ought to wash one another's feet.
>
> (John 13:14)

Most of us have been asked to perform tasks that are unpleasant but necessary to daily living. It was no different during the time of Jesus. Unpaved roads, which also served as the collecting area for sewage and garbage, made the washing of feet a household chore that was relegated to the lowest servant. As the ultimate teacher, Jesus washed the feet of his Apostles to demonstrate what he expected of his followers. The urgency of Jesus's message was intensified because he gave this lesson of loving, humble service the night before he died.

As followers of Jesus, we are called to serve as he did. Every task we perform—even a dreaded, repugnant one—can become a task of love.

What dreaded task in your life could become a task of love?

Great teacher of love, may I embrace all tasks in life with the love you offer.

- To go deeper: Read John 13:1–20.

Jesus of Nazareth: Risen Presence

> The women were terrified and bowed their faces to the ground, but the men [in dazzling clothes] said to them, "Why do you look for the living among the dead? He is not here, but has risen."
>
> (Luke 24:5)

As humans we have a tendency to look for happiness, love, and acceptance in all the wrong places. Following the crowd to be accepted, acquiring possessions to find happiness, or compromising our values to be loved are not uncommon experiences. Jesus's Resurrection teaches us where to find all that we are searching for in our lives— in Christ himself. When the light of Christ's risen presence shines in our lives, we discover we no longer need to be terrified by life's happenings or to be bent to the ground by life's burdens. Jesus's Resurrection calls us to embrace life by discovering that his presence is everywhere.

Where do you look for happiness, love, and acceptance in your life?

Radiant Son, shine in my life and show me where I can find you.

- To go deeper: Read Luke 24:1–12.

Jesus of Nazareth: True Companion

Then their eyes were opened, and they recognized him; and he vanished from their sight.

(Luke 24:31)

Research indicates that walking is one of the best exercises, and its benefits are enhanced when shared with a friend. Young people instinctively know this as they gather to walk to classes or in the local mall. It is also an experience found in Luke's Gospel.

Disappointed and discouraged by the death of Jesus, two of his disciples took off walking and talking as they sought to make sense of what had happened to their beloved Lord. As they journeyed, a stranger joined them and entered their discussion. When they stopped to share a meal, the two disciples recognized the stranger was really Jesus as he broke bread with them. Jesus suddenly disappeared, but his companionship with his disciples lasts forever.

When have you encountered Christ while walking and talking with a friend?

Faithful companion, walk with me and talk to me as I seek you in my life.

• To go deeper: Read Luke 24:13–35.

Simeon: A Man of Spirit

> [Simeon] was righteous and devout, looking forward to the consolation of Israel, and the Holy Spirit rested on him.
>
> (Luke 2:25)

Grandparents play a vital part in the faith life of their grandchildren. Simeon, whom tradition portrays as an elderly, wise, and holy man, was much like a grandparent. Living in Jerusalem and waiting for God's salvation, Simeon longed for the Messiah's coming with patience and hope. Promised that he would not see death before he saw the child of light who would bring salvation to the world, Simeon was a model of devotion and virtue.

We all need witnesses of goodness and perseverance in our lives—wise elders, like Simeon, who have been touched by the Spirit and are willing to wait for God to fulfill a promise. Perseverance is uncommon in a world used to instantaneous response.

How have grandparents been a witness of faith for you?

God, enkindle in me the fire of my ancestors' passion and faith in you.

- To go deeper: Read Luke 2:22–27.

Simeon: A Clear Vision

[Simeon] would not see death before he had seen the Lord's Messiah.

(Luke 2:26)

Hopes, dreams, and planning for the future are essential for humans to live productive and fruitful lives. Some people are quite clear and vocal about what they want to accomplish before they die. Some people know what they will do with their lives; others suffer great pain as they struggle to discover their life's goals.

Simeon's goal in life had been revealed to him by the Holy Spirit—to see the Messiah before he died. We can only speculate on how this promise pervaded his encounters with everyone he saw in his life. Simeon must have wondered, "Might this be the Messiah?" or "Could this be the Christ?" as he met new people throughout his life. Great expectations allowed Simeon to see the world in hope and wonder.

What do you hope to see before you die?

God of great vision, allow me to see what you desire of me before I die.

- To go deeper: Read Luke 2:25–32.

Simeon: Embracing Death

Simeon took [Jesus] in his arms and praised God saying, "Master, now you are dismissing your servant in peace, according to your word."

(Luke 2:28–29)

Ordinarily death is not something most people think about, discuss, or welcome. A tragic accident or a surprise diagnosis may bring the topic to the forefront of our thoughts and feelings, but death is, even then, an unwelcome intruder. Simeon was an exception and, once again, a marvelous role model. As Simeon recognized Christ, he remembered God's promise and blessed God for allowing him to die in peace.

Welcoming death, seeing it as a doorway to all that God has promised, is a challenge and a necessity. The lesson Simeon taught us is so important that the Church uses his prayer (see Luke 2:29–31) as part of night prayer during the Liturgy of the Hours.

What has been your experience of death? Has someone you loved ever died or been close to death? What are your feelings about death?

God of all seasons, be with those in my family who are approaching the winter of their lives. Help them see death as a doorway to life with you.

- To go deeper: Read Luke 2:28–32.

Simeon: Telling It Like It Is!

Then Simeon blessed them and said to [Jesus's] mother Mary, "This child is destined for the falling and the rising of many in Israel, and to be a sign that will be opposed."

(Luke 2:34)

Contrary to what some young people believe, mothers generally want the best for their children. Imagine Mary's puzzlement and concern when she was told that her Son would be opposed and cause the fall of many in Israel. It was only in God's Spirit of love that Simeon was able to speak the truth—to tell it like it was. Simeon first blessed Jesus's parents before he shared the painful prediction.

It is not always easy to be truthful when we have something painful to tell someone. However, when people know we care about them and wish only the best for them, the truth is easier to bear.

How do you prepare when you must share a painful truth with someone?

God, may I always speak the truth out of a loving heart.

• To go deeper: Read Luke 2:33–35.

Anna: Waiting and Ready

> There was also a prophet, Anna the daughter of Phanuel, of the tribe of Asher. She was of a great age.
>
> (Luke 2:36)

Anna was Simeon's female counterpart. She too was elderly and was waiting for the coming of the Messiah. As a prophet, she was called by God to make known divine revelation. As a member of the tribe of Asher, she was from a prosperous lineage. Neither her spoken message nor her inherited wealth seems to matter. All we know about Anna is that she was a prime example of waiting in readiness to receive the Lord.

Those who spend hours preparing to participate in sports, drama, or debate have experienced waiting in readiness on the sidelines until it is their turn to perform. Like Anna, our true worth or wise words may never be known, but our willingness to prepare and wait will inspire and touch the lives of others.

What experiences have you had of waiting for the right time to act or speak?

Patient provider, give me a willing spirit that waits in readiness for you.

- To go deeper: Read Luke 2:36–38.

Anna: Temple Dedication

> [Anna] never left the temple but worshiped there with fasting and prayer night and day.
>
> (Luke 2:37)

It may be hard to imagine Anna's never leaving the Temple and worshiping there day and night. At age eighty-four, Anna had defied statistics and lived as a widow far beyond what was usual for that era in history. Her focus in life was centered on God and practices that kept her close to God.

People who have dedicated their time to weight training in preparation for a sport or who have lived in the practice room in preparation for a musical performance have tasted the determination and dedication of the prophet Anna. Their devotion may even be described in similar terms: he is in the weight room day and night; she practices nonstop. Through God's grace, that kind of dedication can be transferred to a life centered on the Lord.

How is your life dedicated to the Lord?

Lord, help me to focus on one thing—to live with you and for you always.

• To go deeper: Read Luke 2:36–38.

Anna: Cheering the Child

> At that moment [Anna] came, and began to praise
> God and to speak about the child to all who were
> looking for the redemption of Jerusalem.
>
> (Luke 2:38)

Everyone who succumbs to the smile of a little one, the willingness of a child to welcome all, succumbs to the mystery of the life before them. Perhaps this is what Anna was praising God for as she spoke about the child Jesus. Anna was speaking specifically to those who were looking for the redemption of Jerusalem. How can a child show us the way to redemption—perhaps because children possess qualities that are essential to God's being able to work in our lives—openness, trust, joy, and a willingness to grow. Whether we are in our teen years or our twilight years, a child can be our teacher, especially if that child is Christ.

What feelings do children touch in you?

Christ our Lord, child in our midst, teach me your way of growing in wisdom and grace.

• To go deeper: Read Luke 2:36–38.

Samaritan Woman: Braving the Noonday Heat

A Samaritan woman came to draw water.

(John 4:7)

What feels more hurtful than a glance of disapproval or the muffled murmuring of voices critiquing you? Avoiding that experience was the reason the Samaritan woman had braved the noonday heat to get her daily water supply. As a woman with a questionable past, it was painful to face the women of the village who came in the cool of the early morning. In trying to avoid an unpleasant experience, the Samaritan woman met Jesus. As a Jewish man, Jesus should not have spoken to a woman, let alone a Samaritan. Samaritans were detested and widely regarded as unfaithful Jews. In her encounter with Jesus, the woman was drawn into a conversation that ultimately changed her life and the lives of the women she had sought to avoid.

When have others given you a disapproving glance or talked critically about you? How could this be an opportunity to meet Jesus?

Loving Lord, may I encounter you when I am facing unpleasant situations.

• To go deeper: Read John 4:1–15.

Samaritan Woman: Thirsting for God

Jesus said to her, "Give me a drink."

(John 4:7)

"I need a drink of water," is a common request children use at bedtime to avoid going to sleep. They really aren't thirsty. They just don't want to miss what's happening, or they don't want to be alone. When Jesus asked the Samaritan woman for a drink, he also was seeking more than just water. Jesus desired to engage the Samaritan woman in a conversation about her thirst for God. He was able to help her understand that her thirst for water pointed to her greater need for the living water that only God could provide.

We also have many needs—spoken and unspoken, named and unnamed. These needs often point to deeper desires that invite us into conversation with God.

What are my greatest needs at this time in my life? What deeper desires do they indicate?

Lord, may my daily needs lead me to my deepest desire to follow you.

• To go deeper: Read John 4:7–15.

Samaritan Woman: Expanding Our Horizons

"How is it that you, a Jew, ask a drink of me, a woman of Samaria?"

(John 4:9)

Although teenagers are sometimes seen as being rather cliquish, they have no corner on the market. The Samaritan woman showed us her clique mentality when she had difficulty getting beyond what she knew to be true—Jews and Samaritans don't mix or share. Jesus took the woman where she was and invited her to broaden her perspective.

God also asks us to expand our horizons and see people in a new light. Like the Samaritan woman, we don't realize that when we exclude someone, we often miss the gift of God's presence that person could bring into our life.

Who is excluded from your group of friends?

Gathering God, teach me that in you, we are all one. May I move beyond cliques and groups and always be open to your speaking to me through everyone who enters my life.

- To go deeper: Read John 4:9–15.

Samaritan Woman: Revelations

> Jesus said to her, "I am he, the one who is speaking to you."
>
> (John 4:26)

Conversations help clarify what we think and believe; they help us discover who we are and who others are. As the Samaritan woman and Jesus continued their conversation, things eventually became clearer for her. Her interest peaked when Jesus said the water he would provide would offer eternal life. Drawn in by Jesus's words, the woman asked for this water.

We too grow by the conversations we have with others. But we have to have conversations with the right people— people whose knowledge and wisdom can give us new insight and challenge us to be all we can be in service to God. Sometimes those people find us; sometimes we have to find them.

When has a difficult conversation helped to bring clarity to your life or led you to a deeper understanding of Jesus's identity?

Word made flesh, may your presence be revealed in the conversations of my life.

- To go deeper: Read John 4:10–27.

Samaritan Woman: Judging Unfairly

They were astonished that he was speaking with a woman, but no one said, "What do you want?" or, "Why are you speaking with her?"

(John 4:27)

Someone once remarked, "The only exercise some people get is jumping to conclusions." The woman at the well must have felt this as she saw the bewildered disciples who returned from the city. They were astonished to see Jesus visiting with the Samaritan woman, but hesitated in voicing their rash judgments.

Sometimes we see people doing things we may not understand, and we are harsh in our judgments about their motives or intentions. Rarely do we know the whole story about what we see, and we surely want the benefit of the doubt when others see us doing something about which they are unsure.

When have you judged someone prematurely? When have others judged you harshly or unfairly?

Searcher of hearts, please remind me to be gentle in my opinion of others.

- To go deeper: Read John 4:27–38.

Samaritan Woman: True Confessions

> She said to the people, "Come and see a man who told me everything I have ever done! He cannot be the Messiah, can he?"
>
> (John 4:28–30)

When someone knows all about us and still accepts us as a friend, the joy makes us do unusual things. The Samaritan woman was so excited that Jesus didn't condemn her even though he knew her past sins that she left the well without her water jar. Returning to the city, she told the townspeople about this possible Messiah. Having shared this good news of salvation, she then invited the people to "come and see."

People in general don't go around advertising their hidden faults. This woman, however, told those who had condemned her that Jesus knew everything about her and still did not hold it against her. According to some scholars, she could be considered one of the first women apostles, since *apostle* means "one who is sent."

How are you being called to share God's love and acceptance of you?

God, help me invite others to come and see your goodness.

- To go deeper: Read John 4:28–39.

Samaritan Woman: Show Me

> Many Samaritans from the city believed in him because of the woman's testimony.
>
> (John 4:39)

Missouri is a state that proudly boasts its skepticism with the slogan "The Show-Me State," found on their automobile license plates. Samaria was a lot like Missouri; the people also wanted to be shown, not just told. So the people went to Jesus and invited him to come and stay with them. The Scriptures tell us that "many more believed because of his word" (4:41). Excited by this newfound relationship, the townspeople told the Samaritan woman they now believed because of their own experience of the Messiah.

Each of us must come to believe because of our own personal relationship with Jesus, not just because of what others tell us. We must experience Jesus for ourselves and be touched by his life and words.

How are you being invited to believe in Jesus for yourself?

Jesus, help me grow in my relationship with you through prayer and study.

• To go deeper: Read John 4:39–42.

Lazarus: Jesus's Friend

Jesus loved Martha and her sister and Lazarus.

(John 11:5)

Lazarus was an ordinary man who lived in the city of Bethany, which is about two miles from Jerusalem. He had two sisters, Martha and Mary, and all three seemed to be close friends of Jesus. Jesus was a guest in their home. These were Jesus's few close friends, besides the Apostles, that we hear about in the Gospels.

Friendship is a wonderful gift that allows us to enjoy one another's company and to truly be present to one another. Lazarus and Jesus had such a friendship. They cared deeply about one another. So when Lazarus became ill, it was natural for his sisters to call upon Jesus to help. As a good friend, Jesus knew what Lazarus needed most.

How do you depend on your best friends for help in your life?

God, I am grateful for the close friends you have placed in my life. When they ask me for help, let me see their real need.

- To go deeper: Read John 11:1–6.

Lazarus: Illness Strikes

> [Mary's] brother Lazarus was ill. So the sisters sent a message to Jesus, "Lord, he whom you love is ill."
>
> (John 11:2–3)

When faced with the serious illness of their brother, Lazarus, Martha and Mary turned to Jesus for help. They hoped Jesus would return in time and heal their brother of his life-threatening illness. We learn that upon receiving the message, Jesus waited two days before traveling back to Bethany. That span of time must have seemed like an eternity to Mary and Martha.

Illness is a part of life. Some of us may even have a loved one who has had a life-threatening illness. As Christians, we believe Jesus has the power to heal, so, like Mary and Martha, we turn to Jesus for help.

When have you prayed and asked Jesus to heal someone you love who was seriously ill? Did you turn to anyone else?

God, your healing hand can restore life. Please bless and heal those who are seriously ill today.

• To go deeper: Read John 11:1–6.

Lazarus: Death Comes to Lazarus

Then Jesus told [his disciples] plainly, "Lazarus is dead."

(John 11:14)

Even before Jesus started his journey back to Bethany, he informed his disciples that Lazarus was dead. The disciples had to wonder why Jesus was returning then, outside of comforting Martha and Mary. Through the death of Lazarus, Jesus had planned to bring his disciples to a deeper faith.

The death of another person makes real our own mortality. We too will die. Jesus wanted his disciples to be hopeful, not fearful, in the face of death—to deepen their faith, not abandon it. The death of a loved one, even though it is difficult to face and challenging to make sense of, can be an opportunity to deepen our faith in God.

What is your view of death? Is death something to fear or something to embrace to help you grow in faith?

God, as I face the death of people I love, let me feel your presence—your embrace—leading me to deeper faith.

• To go deeper: Read John 11:7–16.

Lazarus: In the Tomb

> When Jesus arrived, he found that Lazarus had already been in the tomb four days.
>
> (John 11:17)

When Jesus neared the village of Bethany, Martha left her house and went to meet Jesus on the road. What a feeling of comfort Martha must have experienced when she came face-to-face with Jesus, a beloved friend. Even so, Martha still questioned why Jesus had not arrived sooner to save her brother.

In the loss of a loved one, the comfort and compassion of friends provides some consolation. Close friends can help us cope with the loss and make sense of the situation, even though we may still question why it had to happen. Faithful friends in these situations are God's gift to us; they are like Jesus coming to comfort Martha and Mary.

How have you been a faithful friend and helped others cope with the loss of a loved one?

God, help me be a person of comfort and hope to those dealing with the death of a loved one.

• To go deeper: Read John 11:17–22.

Lazarus: Resurrection

> Jesus said to her, "Your brother [Lazarus] will rise again." . . . "I am the resurrection and the life."
>
> (John 11:23–25)

Jesus could have kept Lazarus from dying, but instead Jesus used Lazarus's death to talk about Jesus's own Resurrection and the resurrection of all who believe in him. The resurrection that Jesus spoke of was not just something that would happen in the future—it was a present reality. Jesus used Lazarus's resurrection to show his disciples that life after physical death was possible.

As Christians, we believe in life after death and the resurrection of the body—that at the end of time, our bodies will be raised from the dead. We believe that if we are faithful followers, we will live during the time between our physical death and the time of resurrection in the presence of Jesus and God.

What is your image or understanding of life after death? Does it give you hope?

God, we look forward to the day when we will live in your presence, giving you praise day after day.

• To go deeper: Read John 11:23–28.

Lazarus: Jesus Weeps

"Lord, come and see [where Lazarus is buried]."
Jesus began to weep.

(John 11:34–35)

When Jesus saw Lazarus's sister Mary, and all the people
who were with her, mourning the death of Lazarus, Jesus
was deeply moved. He was so moved that Jesus requested
to be shown Lazarus's tomb. When Jesus reached the tomb,
he began to weep—a genuine outpouring of emotion for
someone he had loved.

Expression of emotions is a natural human occurrence.
To weep when someone you love has died is good and
natural. By shedding tears of grief, Jesus expressed his
compassion and solidarity with all who mourned Lazarus.
Great healing can take place when a community gathers
to mourn the dead. That is why we have wakes and
funerals.

How do you express your feeling of loss? Do you
see weeping as a healthy and natural expression of
emotion?

*God, comfort me in my sorrow; show me how to
comfort others in their mourning.*

• To go deeper: Read John 11:28–37.

Lazarus: Raised to Life

[Jesus] cried with a loud voice, "Lazarus, come out!" The dead man came out.

(John 11:43–44)

In dramatic style, Jesus had the stone in front of Lazarus's tomb rolled aside, despite Martha's objection that there would be a stench because the body had already begun to decay. Then Jesus showed God's power over life and death by ordering Lazarus to come out of the tomb. Lazarus emerged from the tomb bound hand and foot in his burial wrappings, and Jesus demanded that he be untied and let go.

The power in this final metaphor is that now raised from the dead, nothing can bind Lazarus anymore; nothing can take away the freedom of life from him. Nothing! Through Jesus's Resurrection, Jesus has conquered death for us as well.

What has kept you bound from living life fully? Do you believe Jesus can free you?

God, call me forth from the fears that bind me and restore me to the fullness of life.

- To go deeper: Read John 11:38–44.

Mary and Martha: Trained in Hospitality

Martha welcomed [Jesus] into her home.

(Luke 10:38)

A large church dedicated to Lazarus stands on the crest of a hill in Bethany overlooking the city of Jerusalem. Scholars seem fairly sure this site had been the home of a brother and two sisters, and that it possibly was the home of Jesus's good friends Lazarus, Martha, and Mary. The Scriptures mention Jesus's visiting them several times but, in reality, he probably visited his friends more often than is recorded. As part of their education, Martha and Mary would have been trained in the fine art of hospitality. Food, refreshment, and a warm welcome would have greeted Jesus's arrival.

Attending to the needs of others is a key to good hospitality and to being a follower of Christ. When we attend to the needs of others, we are tending to the needs of Christ.

How do you make your friends feel welcome?

Jesus, may I see your face in those who are in need and those who come to my door.

• To go deeper: Read Matthew 25:31–40.

Martha: Good Impressions

"Lord, do you not care that my sister has left me to do all the work by myself? Tell [Mary] then to help me."

(Luke 10:40)

It is possible that Martha was older than Mary, for she appears to have taken charge of the house and hospitality. Because unmarried women would seldom go out in public, we can assume Jesus was first a friend of Lazarus, who brought Jesus home for dinner one day. Lazarus may have shared his excitement in meeting the traveling teacher, and Martha wanted to make a good impression. She was upset when Mary was more concerned with listening to Jesus's stories than with helping her.

We often are busy doing things for the wrong reasons. Like Martha, we may be more concerned with making a good impression than in really being attentive to those before us.

When have you taken time out from your busy schedule to really listen to someone?

Jesus, like Martha I am busy with many things. Help me stop and listen to your voice.

• To go deeper: Read Luke 10:38–42.

Mary: Deep Devotion

> Mary was the one who anointed the Lord with perfume and wiped his feet with her hair.
>
> (John 11:2)

Mary of Bethany possibly was the youngest in the family. She appears to have been a good listener and devoted to God's word. Jesus was pleased with Mary's piercing attention to his words as she sat and listened carefully to his teachings during his visits. It was Mary who, in her eagerness to express affection and reverence for Jesus, poured out precious perfume on the Lord and wiped his feet with her hair. She loved Jesus and searched for a way to express her devotion.

People often go to great lengths to show their devotion to a particular sports team by following the team's every move in the media and buying team clothing and accessories. We are called to be just as devoted to God by listening to and following God's word.

How can you be more devoted to reading and following God's word?

Lord Jesus, may my devotion to your word lead me to serve others.

• To go deeper: Read John 12:1–8.

Mary and Martha: Prayer or Service

> But the Lord answered [Martha], . . . "Mary has chosen the better part."
>
> (Luke 10:41–42)

Jesus seems to have defended Mary when Martha complained that her sister was not helping her with the household duties. Mary had sat listening to Jesus and drinking in everything he had to say. Yet it was Martha who had organized the welcome and the meal to receive Jesus at their house.

Folks still argue about what is better, to pray or to work in service of the Lord's people. Great saints throughout history have even established religious communities that devote themselves exclusively to either contemplative prayer or active service. The truth is that both are needed for a healthy Church. At certain times in our lives, we communicate best with God in quiet prayer, while at other times, we meet God in service to others.

When have you been led to quiet reflection? to serve others?

Dear Lord, may my actions always be rooted in prayer.

• To go deeper: Read Psalm 84.

Mary and Martha: Believing in Jesus

> So the sisters sent a message to Jesus, "Lord, he whom you love is ill."
>
> (John 11:3)

Mary and Martha must have been frantic as their brother worsened and grew weaker. They sent Jesus a message that Lazarus was gravely ill, sick unto death. But Jesus had another plan, one that required faith, and decided to stay two more days before going to see his good friend. Jesus saw beyond the immediate danger of Lazarus's pending death to God's plan to save not only Lazarus from death but all of God's people.

Sometimes we feel that the Lord is far away when we need God most. We may be facing an illness or the loss of a friend or family member. It is then that we need to have faith in God's plan for us.

When have you had to wait for Jesus to answer your request for help?

Lord, I believe you have a plan for every situation, even though I don't see it. Help me, Lord, to believe like Martha.

• To go deeper: Read John 11:1–16.

Mary and Martha: Death and Resurrection

"Lord, if [only] you had been here, my brother would not have died."

(John 11:21)

Martha and Mary waited for Jesus to come—but he didn't! Lazarus grew weaker, the illness got worse, and still Jesus didn't come. When Lazarus did die, it was another four days before Jesus even arrived in Bethany to mourn the death of his friend and to comfort Martha and Mary. Martha's words, that Lazarus would not have had to die if only Jesus had been there, set the stage for Jesus's discourse on the Paschal mystery—that those who believe in Jesus, even though they may suffer and die, will be given new life in Christ.

Amid suffering and loss, we also have a tendency to say "if only . . ." in an attempt to make sense of the situation. We don't immediately see that God has a plan and that out of suffering and death will come new life.

When, after facing a difficult situation, have you been tempted to say "if only . . ."?

Jesus, during times of suffering and loss, help me remember you are leading me to everlasting life.

• To go deeper: Read John 11:17–27.

Mary and Martha: Seeing the Glory of God

> Jesus said to [Martha], "Did I not tell you that if you believed, you would see the glory of God?"
>
> (John 11:40)

Martha's and Mary's prayers were answered. Their brother, Lazarus, who had been dead was now alive. What great joy! The sisters did not have to wait until the final resurrection to experience God's glory. God's glory was standing right before them in the person of Jesus Christ. Because they believed, they experienced God's promise of new life.

During the Church's funeral liturgy, when the body of the deceased is prepared for burial, we ask the Lord to give us the same consolation Jesus gave Mary and Martha—that our belief in Christ will lead us to seeing God's eternal glory.

When has believing in Christ's Resurrection given you hope in times of sorrow?

Lord of the resurrection and everlasting life, give me the faith to believe in you.

• To go deeper: Read John 11:38–44.

Nicodemus: Under Cover of Darkness

A Pharisee named Nicodemus, a leader of the Jews
. . . came to Jesus by night.

(John 3:1–2)

Darkness can generate courage or fear. Covered by the anonymity of shadows, some people find bravery to do things in secret. As a highly respected teacher of the Jewish Law, Nicodemus experienced both emotions in his moonlight meeting with Jesus. Fearful of what others would think if he was seen in the daylight visiting with Jesus, he conjured up the courage to come to Jesus at night.

Like Nicodemus, consciousness of what others think sometimes determines the decisions we make. We too may be afraid to show public displays of our faith and prefer to come to Jesus under the cover of darkness. Day or night, Christ accepts us whenever we come to him.

When have you done a good deed in the daylight?

Giver of courage, strengthen my heart to do what is right in the daylight of your love.

• To go deeper: Read John 3:1–10.

Nicodemus: Recognizing the Real

"Rabbi, we know that you are a teacher who has come from God; for no one can do these signs that you do apart from the presence of God."

(John 3:2)

Made with real butter, real lemons, or real leather are bylines used to market products. We want and recognize the real. Everything about Christ was real; Nicodemus recognized and acknowledged this as he bravely engaged Christ in conversation.

We learn to be real by experiencing people who are true to their convictions. Coaches, grandparents, teachers, and parents play a major role in helping us realize the effect God can have on our lives. Allowing Christ's real presence to touch our lives gives us the strength and courage to let Christ influence our daily decisions. Then Christ's goodness will radiate from us, making us real.

Whom do you consider to be real and true to their convictions?

Jesus, may your goodness shine through me, making me real.

• To go deeper: Read John 3:2–15.

Nicodemus: **God at the Gridiron**

"God so loved the world that he gave his only Son, so that everyone who believes in him may not perish but may have eternal life."

(John 3:16)

It is the rare football game that doesn't have some dedicated Christian displaying a reference to this Scripture passage. Little did Nicodemus realize that the answer to his question to Jesus would be immortalized in such a fashion. What a relief it must have been for Nicodemus to hear that God loved the world and that Jesus became human so all people could have eternal life.

The teen years are often filled with a swirl of questions, concerns, and doubts: "Am I loved?" "Will I make it?" "Does anyone care?" In the middle of the night, Nicodemus received the answer yes to these questions. It is wonderful to be reminded of this by loyal football fans who bring God to the gridiron.

How has God's love touched your life?

Touch my life with your love, Lord, that I may know the power of your presence.

• To go deeper: Read John 3:16–21.

Nicodemus: Finding the Light

Those who do what is true come to the light.

(John 3:21)

Nicodemus came to Jesus in darkness and departed with an assurance that his search for the truth had led him to the light. The heaviness of his fear was replaced by the light of faith. Jesus spoke of the need to be born again in Baptism, and Nicodemus emerged from his encounter with Jesus touched by the truth of God's love and able to live a new life. Nicodemus now had the courage to witness to the Lord in the daylight. He spoke to the Jewish council on behalf of Jesus and helped prepare Jesus's body for burial.

Like Nicodemus, many of us know the joy of having the Lord's light touch our lives. Participating in a Confirmation retreat or helping those in need can affect our lives and enlighten us to the truth of God's love.

When has an insight of God's truth led you to the light of God's love?

Lord, light of my life, show me the way to your truth.

• To go deeper: Read John 7:45–52, 19:38–42.

Zacchaeus: Vertically Challenged

> [Zacchaeus] was trying to see who Jesus was, but
> . . . could not, because he was short in stature.
>
> (Luke 19:3)

Modern comparisons would liken Zacchaeus, the head Jewish tax collector for the Romans, to today's Internal Revenue Service. The difference is that the Romans demanded a certain amount of taxes from the Jews, but allowed people like Zacchaeus to collect more and pocket the difference. It appears Zacchaeus was skilled in his job because he was rich, but his wealth did not solve all his problems.

Most of us recognize we have limitations to overcome. The inability to accept limitations can drive some to seek power by dominating or demeaning others. Perhaps Zacchaeus's choice to collect taxes gave him a way to deal with his limitations.

What is your greatest limitation? How do you deal with it?

Lord, teach me to move beyond all that keeps me from you.

- To go deeper: Read Luke 19:1–10.

Zacchaeus: Out on a Limb

> So [Zacchaeus] ran ahead and climbed a sycamore
> tree to see [Jesus].
>
> (Luke 19:4)

Dedication and determination, plus a willingness to appear somewhat foolish, made all the difference in Zacchaeus's life. Zacchaeus was willing to do anything—even go out on a limb—to see who this Jesus was. Running and tree climbing were not activities that well-respected Jewish men engaged in during that time. Zacchaeus broke rank with the customs of the day and did what his heart told him to do.

Young people today face many unwritten expectations as to what they can or cannot do if they are to be accepted by their peers. Participation in church-related activities or talking about your faith can seem like going out on a limb. The feeling of being alone and unsupported can be frightening. We need to remember that Jesus is there with us.

When has being a follower of Jesus taken you out on a limb?

Lord, may I do whatever is necessary to see you in my life.

• To go deeper: Read Luke 19:1–10.

Zacchaeus: Jesus as Guest

> [Jesus] said to him, "Zacchaeus, hurry and come down, for I must stay at your house today."
>
> (Luke 19:5)

The human heart aches to be acknowledged—especially when it is beating with desire. Zacchaeus was determined to see who this Jesus was, and Jesus would not disappoint him. In fact, some would see Jesus as a bit brazen as he invited himself to be a guest in Zacchaeus's home. It was beyond anything Zacchaeus expected. Jesus even conveyed urgency as he told Zacchaeus to hurry. God is never outdone in generosity; if we take the first step, God will come to meet us.

The idealism of youth can leave some teens believing that following the Lord requires doing big and bold things to change the world. The life of Zacchaeus is a reminder that first we must open the door of our hearts and let Jesus in. The rest will follow.

How are you being called to let Jesus into your life?

Come, Lord Jesus, stay in the home of my life forever.

• To go deeper: Read Luke 19:1–10.

Woman Caught in Adultery: Facing the Consequences

"Teacher [Jesus], this woman was caught in the very act of committing adultery."

(John 7:4)

The woman, clad in clothing that revealed way too much, stood before a group of scribes and Pharisees who presented her before Jesus and accused her of adultery. She knew the consequences! The law of Moses prescribed that such a woman be killed in public view—death by suffocation or injury as the authorities pushed her from the top of a hill and heaved boulders and rocks down upon her. She couldn't plead anything. She had been caught.

Standing before her accusers and Jesus, the woman came face-to-face with what she had done. Facing the consequences of our actions is never easy. Even though we may be condemned by others, Jesus is always ready to forgive.

Have you ever been caught doing something wrong? What were the consequences of your actions?

Help me, Lord, to own up to my mistakes and accept the consequences.

• To go deeper: Read John 7:45—8:6.

Woman Caught in Adultery: Stone Throwing

"Let anyone among you who is without sin be the first to throw a stone at her."

(John 8:7)

For some time, Jesus just ignored the crowd and wrote in the sand with his finger while the crowd pushed, yelled, and accused the woman. Finally, Jesus stood up and told the crowd that anyone who had not sinned could stone her. With that, Jesus bent over again and continued writing. As he wrote, one by one the woman's accusers began to slip away from the crowd. Could it have been the sins of those in the crowd that Jesus wrote down?

It is easy to get caught up in a crowd mentality and point the finger at someone who is obviously in the wrong and causing scandal. Before throwing stones at someone else, we need to stop and remember that we too are sinners, whether or not our sins are obvious to others.

When have you judged another and failed to see your own faults?

Merciful Jesus, may I show others the mercy you have shown me.

• To go deeper: Read Psalm 51.

Woman Caught in Adultery: Second Chances

> Jesus said, "Neither do I condemn you. Go your way, and . . . do not sin again."
>
> (John 8:11)

The wretched, guilty woman was left alone with the young rabbi from Nazareth. What was she to do? The mob wasn't far away. Maybe they would come back and stone her to death after all. Then Jesus stood up and looked at her. He began to speak to her kindly, telling her that no one had condemned her and that she was free to go. The woman must have stood there in disbelief. No one condemned her? And Jesus, despite her guilt, only told her to go and change her ways.

Instead of condemning the woman to death, Jesus gave her a second chance at life. We also have been given a second chance through Jesus's death on the cross. Jesus died for our sins once and for all. In gratitude, we turn from our sins toward life.

When has someone forgiven you and given you a second chance?

Thank you, Jesus, for giving me a second chance at life.

- To go deeper: Read John 8:7–11.

Woman Caught in Adultery: Tears of Mercy

> "Daughters of Jerusalem, do not weep for me, but weep for yourselves and for your children."
>
> (Luke 23:28)

We never learn the adulterous woman's name. Jesus never even named her sin. He didn't preach at her, warn her, or threaten her. He simply told her to change, to do good instead of evil. This woman could well have been in the great crowd of people, many of them women, who wept at seeing Jesus on the way to his death on Calvary. Perhaps Jesus even recognized her in the crowd when he told the women not to weep for him.

Tears are cleansing, especially tears of repentance. Even though some people want to put sins in categories from bad to worse, there is no sin God cannot forgive. Jesus sees and hears the evidence accusing each of us, but he forgives us and urges us to change our ways.

Have you ever cried tears of repentance?

God, give me a longing for mercy so that I too might show compassion and forgiveness.

• To go deeper: Read Luke 23:27–34.

Lydia: Church Leader

> A certain woman named Lydia, a worshiper of
> God, was listening to [Paul and his companions].
>
> (Acts of the Apostles 16:14)

Paul, the great missionary, took the Gospel message
far and wide. His journeys are recorded in the Acts of
the Apostles. It was in Philippi that Paul first encountered
Lydia. Lydia was an independently wealthy woman who
ran a very successful business dealing with purple dye
and fabric. On the Sabbath, Paul came across Lydia and
a group of women gathered by a river for prayer. Paul
spoke to them of Jesus and the growing Church. Lydia
listened intently to Paul's words and opened her heart to
the Lord. She became the first European convert.

Women like Lydia were instrumental in the formation
of the early Church. It was not unusual for a woman,
especially a wealthy woman, to lead the early Christian
communities in prayer and worship.

What women do you consider to be leaders of the
Church today?

*God, help me appreciate the women who lead and
serve my parish community.*

- To go deeper: Read Acts of the Apostles 16:11–14.

Lydia: Generous Woman

> [Lydia] urged us, saying, "If you have judged me to be faithful to the Lord, come and stay at my home."
>
> (Acts of the Apostles 16:15)

Lydia was probably a widow (because a husband is not mentioned) who cared for a large household. When Paul convinced Lydia to accept Jesus as the Son of God, her whole household was baptized with her. This gracious and generous lady put not only her wealth but also everyone who lived with and worked for her at the disposal of Paul and the Apostles.

Lydia gave more than just her heart over to Christ; she entrusted everything she had in the Church. Many churches exist today because of the sacrifices that faith-filled people have made over the centuries—giving both time and money so the Church can continue to thrive and grow.

How do you support your parish church, Catholic school, or youth group?

Lord, bless those who give time and money to support my parish.

• To go deeper: Read Philippians 4:1–20.

Lydia: Baptized in Christ

[Lydia] and her household were baptized.

(Acts of the Apostles 16:15)

Lydia deserves to be remembered not for the royal purple dye she knew how to produce but because she was a royal woman, a woman willing to be dressed in the royal purple Christ wore to his death. In choosing to be baptized and in opening her home and fortune to Paul and his group of evangelists, Lydia put not only her livelihood at risk but also her very life. She had found a truth, a cause, and a faith she could believe in and hold fast to.

Being baptized in Christ means we have to be willing to risk everything to spread the good news of God's love—even if that means risking our very life. We are called to a royal priesthood, a willingness to sacrifice everything for Christ.

What are you willing to risk in order to make God's love known?

God, may I be worthy to wear the royal robes of your sacrificial love.

- To go deeper: Read Philippians 1:1–14.

Peter: Catcher of People

> "Do not be afraid; from now on you will be catching people."
>
> (Luke 5:10)

Peter, known as Simon, was born on the north coast of the Sea of Galilee in the city of Bethsaida, which means "house of the fisherman." By the time Peter met Jesus, he was married and living in Capernaum, just a few miles west of Bethsaida. Peter and his brother Andrew owned a fishing company with James and John, the sons of Zebedee. Peter's astonishing journey as Jesus's disciple led him to catching people instead of fish. He became a great missionary for Jesus and died a martyr in Rome.

Jesus promised Peter that his life as a disciple would be much more interesting than his life as a fisherman. Jesus also calls us to share the Gospel message and offers us an astonishing journey. The risks are high, but the rewards are grander.

What astonishing life journey is Jesus inviting you to?

Jesus, give me the courage to journey with you.

- To go deeper: Read Luke 5:1–11.

Peter: Called to Be a Disciple

And [Jesus] said to [Peter and Andrew], "Follow me, and I will make you fish for people."

(Matthew 4:19)

Matthew tells us that Peter and Andrew followed Jesus immediately. In fact, they accompanied Jesus in recruiting their business partners James and John. There was a cost in following Jesus—leaving behind good careers as fishermen—that his first disciples eventually accepted because what they gained far exceeded their wildest dreams.

Being a disciple of Jesus demands that we make sacrifices, that we leave behind our dreams to follow God's dream. It means doing or not doing certain things because of our commitment to a Christian lifestyle. But ultimately following Jesus is not a matter of giving up something but rather of embracing a lifestyle that brings about good.

How have you responded to the call to follow Jesus?

Jesus, may my response to your call be a resounding and immediate yes!

• To go deeper: Read Matthew 4:18–22.

Peter: Recognizing God's Power

> But when Simon Peter saw it, he fell down at Jesus's knees, saying, "Go away from me, Lord, for I am a sinful man!"
>
> (Luke 5:8)

In the story line of Luke's Gospel, Jesus was at sea when he called Peter and some of the other disciples to follow him. The fishermen had not caught anything all night, but Jesus told them to go out to deeper water and cast their nets. Their nets were filled to capacity. Peter protested that he was a sinner and not worthy to follow Jesus. Jesus, however, looked beyond Peter's sinfulness and saw someone who recognized God's power in his life.

At our Baptism, each of us is called to follow Jesus and to recognize God's power in our lives. Even though we are sinners, Jesus looks into our hearts and sees our full potential as his followers.

What potential does Jesus see in you? Where do you recognize God's power in your life?

God, you probe me and you know me. In humility I give myself to your mission.

- To go deeper: Read Luke 5:1–11.

Peter: Person of Faith and Doubt

So Peter got out of the boat, started walking on the water, and came toward Jesus. But when he noticed the strong wind, he became frightened.

(Matthew 14:29–30)

Peter's strong faith made it possible for him to get out of the boat and walk on the water toward Jesus. When Peter was focused on Jesus, he could continue to walk on the water. When doubt crept in and Peter lost his focus on Jesus, he became frightened and began to sink. In his doubt, Peter cried out and asked Jesus to save him. Both convicted faith and conflicted human doubt existed within Peter.

Like Peter, we also are a mix of faith and doubt all rolled up together. As we grow in our faith, new doubts arise for us. At the same time, our doubts have the potential to lead us to a deeper faith in Jesus.

How are you a person of deep faith? What doubts do you have?

God, increase my faith as I encounter new questions of faith.

• To go deeper: Read Matthew 14:22–33.

Peter: The Rock Foundation

"And I tell you, you are Peter and on this rock I will build my church."

(Matthew 16:18)

Jesus blessed Peter with these words after Peter proclaimed his belief in Jesus as the Messiah. Jesus recognized that it was God the Father who had revealed this to Peter. It was upon Peter's rock-solid faith that the Church of Jesus Christ was built. Jesus guaranteed that God's revelation would endure the test of time by entrusting Peter with the protection of this truth.

The Greek words the author of the Gospel uses, *petros* (Peter) and *petra* (rock), are a play on words that both refer to a foundation stone for building. The foundation of the Christian faith is built upon the truth that Jesus is the Messiah and upon Peter as the head of the Church. As Christians, we continue to build upon that foundation today.

How does your life give witness to Jesus as the Messiah?

God, fashion my faith to be a rock in the foundation of your Church today.

• To go deeper: Read Matthew 16:13–20.

Peter: Denial

> Then Peter remembered what Jesus had said: "Before the cock crows, you will deny me three times."
>
> (Matthew 26:75)

At the Passover meal, when Jesus foretold that Peter would deny him, Peter defended himself by saying he would never desert Jesus—even if it meant he would have to die. Only hours later, in fear for his life, Peter denied Jesus three times in the courtyard of the high priest Caiaphas, where Jesus was being held prisoner.

Peter was good at putting up a front—a tough act—in vowing never to desert Jesus. But when faced with the reality of death, the facade broke and Peter did exactly what he had said he wouldn't do. In recognizing his fault, Peter wept. We often don't live up to our ideals and find ourselves, like Peter, doing what we say we wouldn't do.

When have you failed to be faithful to God? How have you shown sorrow?

God, when I fail to be faithful because of fear, give me the grace to be remorseful.

• To go deeper: Read Matthew 26:69–75.

Peter: Do You Love Me?

Jesus said to Simon Peter, "Simon son of John, do you love me more than these?"

(John 21:15)

After Jesus's Resurrection, Peter was given the chance to make good on his promise to never desert Jesus. In a profound dialogue, Jesus asked Peter three times, "Do you love me?"—a clear parallel to Peter's earlier threefold denial of Jesus. Each time, Peter proclaimed his love for Jesus.

John's Gospel tells us that Peter felt hurt when Jesus asked the question a third time. Jesus knew Peter had never stopped loving him, but it was Peter who needed to say it. Jesus was giving Peter a chance to reaffirm his love for him and to demonstrate his love for Christ by caring for the Church.

Do you give those who love you a second chance to express their love if they offend you?

God, I love you completely. Forgive me for the times I act in ways that are contrary to that love.

- To go deeper: Read John 21:4–19.

Mary Magdalene: Driving Out the Demons

> The twelve were with him, as well as some women who had been cured of evil spirits and infirmities: Mary, called Magdalene, from whom seven demons had gone out.
>
> (Luke 8:1–2)

It is part of human nature to be naturally attracted to those who are strong, perfect, and independent. Jesus was just the opposite. He was attracted to those who were sick, weak, or living less than perfect lives. They were also the people who were attracted to Jesus. Mary, from the Galilean fishing village of Magdala, was one of those persons. We don't know what her struggles, or demons, in life were. We know only that the Lord gave her strength to turn and follow God.

No matter what our demons in life are—loneliness, fear, depression, illness, disabilities—we can be sure that Jesus embraces us just as we are. He has the power to release us and give us the strength to follow him.

What are some of the demons you struggle with?

Lord, release me from my demons and help me follow you.

- To go deeper: Read Luke 8:1–3.

Mary Magdalene: The Least Likely

> Now after [Jesus] rose early on the first day of the
> week, he appeared first to Mary Magdalene.
>
> (Mark 16:9)

Mary Magdalene had two strikes against her: first, she
was a woman; second, her life hadn't been perfect.
Somehow that didn't matter to Jesus because she was the
first person he appeared to following his Resurrection—as
told in the Gospel of John. One might expect that Jesus
would have first gone to his mother or at least to John, his
beloved disciple. But instead, he chose Mary Magdalene
to be the first to witness and proclaim that Jesus had been
raised.

As you look at your classmates, friends, and family,
whom do you consider the least likely to be chosen by
God to proclaim the Gospel message? God often chooses
those we would reject to proclaim God's message of love
and peace.

When have you felt like the "least likely" to be
chosen?

*God of grand vision, help me see as you do and not
reject those you have chosen to spread your word.*

• To go deeper: Read Mark 16:9–11.

Mary Magdalene: At the Cross

> Meanwhile, standing near the cross of Jesus were his mother, and his mother's sister, Mary the wife of Clopas, and Mary Magdalene.
>
> (John 19:25)

Friendship is sealed in the moment when "staying with" is chosen over "walking away." Mary Magdalene was that kind of friend to Jesus. When all the men had left, it was a few women who remained as friends to the end around the cross.

Learning how to stay with someone in their hour of need is a vital part of cultivating lifelong friendships. That hour of need, or cross, may be the divorce of parents, a major illness, or a bad decision whose ramifications may last a lifetime. We may also find, like Mary, that those who remain are few in number. But God is always at our side, and Mary shows us how to remain faithful to the end.

Who has stayed with you in your time of need?

Dear Lord, faithful friend, give me the strength to stay with friends in their hour of need.

- To go deeper: Read John 19:17–27.

Mary Magdalene: Love Is in the Details

> Mary Magdalene and Mary the mother of Joses saw where the body [of Jesus] was laid.
>
> (Mark 15:47)

Some experiences in life are so monumental that every detail is noticed. Jesus's presence had such an impact on Mary Magdalene's life that all the details of his death were vital to her. She even watched to see where he was laid to rest. The love Jesus had shown her called forth a reciprocal love from Mary Magdalene, and she was not about to leave him.

As we begin to experience friendship and love, we also become aware of the details surrounding the ones who have touched our hearts. We become conscious of what they like and dislike, where they spend time, and whom they hang out with. Every detail becomes a treasured memory.

When has an experience of loving someone helped you pay attention to details?

Loving Lord, grant me the grace to tend to the details love requires.

- To go deeper: Read Mark 15:42–47.

Mary Magdalene: In Times of Loss

> [Joseph Arimathea] then . . . went away. Mary Magdalene and the other Mary were there, sitting opposite the tomb.
>
> (Matthew 27:60–61)

Strategies for coping with loss are as varied as the individuals who face it. Mary Magdalene had just lost her dearest friend. How could she go on without him? The rest of Jesus's followers had left, but Mary Magdalene remained at the gravesite and waited.

Loss comes in many ways: divorce may bring loss of life with our parents as we know it, the death of a friend or grandparent may bring loss of an understanding confidant, moving may bring loss of treasured friends. The temptation may be to fill our emptiness with dangerous diversions like drugs, alcohol, or inappropriate behavior. Mary Magdalene teaches us how to remain with the emptiness of loss and not run away.

What is your response to the losses in life?

God, strengthen me in my time of loss that I may turn to you in hope.

- To go deeper: Read Matthew 27:57–61.

Mary Magdalene: The Body of Christ

> When the sabbath was over, Mary Magdalene,
> and Mary the mother of James, and Salome bought
> spices, so that they might go and anoint him.
>
> (Mark 16:1)

Because of their love for Jesus, Mary Magdalene and her companions rushed to reverence his dead body as soon as Jewish Law would allow. Following their tradition, they anointed his body with richly scented oil.

Professional athletes and Olympic participants are expected to pay attention to their bodies. Exercise and nutrition are vital to who they are and what they choose to do with their lives. For many young people, this is a value yet to be learned. Eating healthy foods, exercising, and taking care of your physical well-being should be important priorities. Our bodies are a gift from God, and we need to care for them so we can do good deeds and witness to God's presence in the world.

How do you show honor and respect to your body? How do you honor and respect others?

Source of life, teach me to reverence all of life.

- To go deeper: Read Mark 16:1–8.

Mary Magdalene: Called by Name

> Jesus said to her, "Mary!" She turned and said to him in Hebrew, "Rabbouni!" (which means Teacher).
>
> (John 20:16)

Nothing touches us more deeply than hearing our name lovingly and tenderly spoken. Mary Magdalene's spirits were raised at hearing the voice of her teacher. Having remained at Jesus's tomb weeping when all the others had left, Mary's heart must have been breaking in grief as she tried to make sense of the empty grave. Upon hearing Jesus gently speak her name, all her questions and grief disappeared. She couldn't help but run to tell the others the Good News.

Being called by name can evoke different responses. Hearing our name spoken in love can propel us to respond in kindness, whereas hearing our name spoken in condemnation can cause us to be defensive.

How do you feel when someone lovingly calls your name?

God of all names, teach me to treasure the ways you call me.

- To go deeper: Read John 20:11–18.

Paul: Religious Zeal

> I advanced in Judaism beyond many among my people of the same age, for I was far more zealous for the traditions of my ancestors.

> (Galatians 1:14)

A tent maker by trade, Paul's Jewish name was Saul. But because Paul spent most of his life preaching in an area of the Roman Empire outside of Israel, he went by his Roman name. Paul was born in Tarsus, renowned as a center for education. However, Paul received his Jewish education in Jerusalem under Gamaliel, a leading teacher of the Law. Paul was a Pharisee who, out of zeal (passion) for his Jewish faith, persecuted Jesus's followers. After a dramatic conversion, Paul redirected his religious zeal and took the Gospel message to the world.

Conviction in following what we know to be true is at the heart of religious zeal. But, like Paul, our zeal can either lead us to persecute others or to love them.

On a scale of one to ten, how zealous are you about your faith?

God, I pray that my zeal for you will lead me to love and care for others.

- To go deeper: Read Acts of the Apostles 7:54–60.

Paul: Persecutor of Christians

> Saul was ravaging the church by entering house after house; dragging off both men and women . . . to prison.
>
> (Acts of the Apostles 8:3)

Convinced that following the teachings of Jesus was wrong, Paul pursued the early Christians and put them in jail. He was even present at and approved the stoning of Stephen, the first Christian martyr. Paul would not allow anything to get in the way of his convictions.

As a Pharisee, Paul lived his life by the letter of the law. He saw himself as a defender of the faith. We know from Jesus that living our faith goes beyond the letter of the law to the spirit of the law. Having conviction in our religious beliefs and defending them when necessary is important, but in doing so we must not lose sight of God's love at the heart of those beliefs.

When has following the letter of the law caused you to ignore God's law of love?

God, help me to live my faith with conviction and to respect the beliefs of others.

• To go deeper: Read Acts of the Apostles 8:1–4.

Paul: A Profound Conversion

> [Saul] heard a voice saying to him, "Saul, Saul, why do you persecute me?"
>
> (Acts of the Apostles 9:4)

It was on his way to Damascus that Paul was struck down by God and blinded. A brilliant light from heaven surrounded Paul, and he heard a voice accusing Paul of persecuting him. When Paul asked who it was he was persecuting, Paul was astounded to discover that in persecuting Christians he was actually persecuting Jesus. Afterward, Paul underwent a profound conversion and was baptized.

Dramatic conversions happen even today—not by being struck down by a great light, but by being enlightened. Once we have become aware of a new truth, we cannot go back to our previous way of living. We must move ahead, growing stronger in this new way of seeing the world.

When has a new awareness led you to act differently?

God, you continually call me to conversion; let me be open to seeing your truth.

- To go deeper: Read Acts of the Apostles 9:1–19.

Paul: Theologian

> They were attempting to kill [Paul]. When the believers learned of it . . . they sent him off to Tarsus.
>
> (Acts of the Apostles 9:29–30)

After his conversion, Paul began to preach, but when it became too dangerous, he was sent to Tarsus. Tradition tells us that Paul spent several years reflecting on Jesus's life, Passion, death, and Resurrection. Through prayer, study, and reflection, Paul developed a theology that served as the foundation of his preaching of the Gospel of Jesus.

We need to reflect on the mysteries of our faith to grow in understanding and to know which direction to take in life. Two great tools to guide our reflection are the Bible and the Catechism of the Catholic Church. You may want to seek out youth-friendly versions of these.

How much time do you spend each week in learning about your faith?

God, help me create time in my busy life to study and reflect on my faith.

• To go deeper: Read Acts of the Apostles 9:19–31.

Paul: Missionary

[Paul] had opened a door of faith for the Gentiles.

(Acts of the Apostles 14:27)

Known as the apostle to the Gentiles (non-Jews), Paul was a leader in taking the Gospel message beyond Israel. With his trusted companions—Barnabas, John Mark, Timothy, Priscilla, and Aquila—Paul traveled extensively and took the Good News to the world. Paul was both welcomed and opposed, but he never wavered or grew weary in his missionary vigor. Through his letters, Paul kept in touch with the various communities he helped form—instructing, affirming, and encouraging them to live the Christian faith.

As Christians, we are called to continue the mission of bringing the Good News of Jesus to the people we meet each day. It is what we do, not what we say, that proclaims God's message most clearly. Sometimes we may be the only Gospel some people encounter.

When have you been a missionary for the Gospel of Jesus?

God, do not let my fear get in the way of being your presence in the world.

- To go deeper: Read Acts of the Apostles 14:1–28.

Paul: The Journey to Rome

If God is for us, who is against us?

(Romans 8:31)

In Paul's last trip to Jerusalem to say farewell before leaving to preach in Spain, he was arrested by the Romans. As a Roman citizen, Paul exercised his right to appeal his case before the emperor in Rome. After a tumultuous trip across the Mediterranean Sea, Paul arrived in Rome around AD 60 and was kept under house arrest. While there, he continued to preach and strengthen the Christian Church. According to tradition, Paul was beheaded outside the walls of the city. The Church recognizes Paul as a genuine hero of the faith.

Paul never made it to Spain, but he made a great difference in Rome. It is not uncommon to experience detours in life and end up somewhere unexpected. It is what we do with the detour that makes all the difference.

How have you used unexpected situations in your life for good?

God, may I always have dreams that take me beyond myself.

- To go deeper: Read Acts of the Apostles 28:11–30.

Paul: Legacy of Love

> [Love] bears all things, believes all things, hopes all things, endures all things.
>
> (1 Corinthians 13:7)

Paul preached that the central message of Jesus Christ was love. Without love, no amount of faith or religious piety has any meaning. Paul emphasized that salvation is gained through God's grace and through faith in Jesus. These understandings of Christian love have inspired and challenged theologians throughout history.

Paul's legacy lives on in the Church today as it strives to live out the implications of true Christian love. Many homilies have been preached, many books have been written, and many debates have occurred in the pursuit of fully grasping the ramifications of Christian love. It seems so simple—love God with your whole being and love your neighbor as yourself—but it is so hard to do.

How do you try to live God's commandment to love?

God, help me live your commandment to love each day.

- To go deeper: Read 1 Corinthians 13:1–13.

Timothy: A Believer's Son

There was a disciple named Timothy, the son of a Jewish woman who was a believer.

(Acts of the Apostles 16:1)

We first meet Timothy, a disciple of Paul, in Lystra, where he lived with his devout Jewish mother, who had become a believer, and his Greek father, a non-Jew. After hearing the Christian community praise Timothy for his faith, Paul invited Timothy to accompany him on his missionary journeys. Paul's pattern was to preach first in the synagogues, so having Timothy, a Jewish believer, with him helped in winning Jewish converts.

Paul's work as a missionary was built on the foundation of the prophets and the faithful people of Israel. As Christians, our roots start in Judaism—we belong to a long family history of faithful believers.

Do you know when you were baptized? What is the faith history of your family?

Lord, help me accept and appreciate the faith that has been handed on to me.

• To go deeper: Read Acts of the Apostles 16:1–5.

Timothy: Leader and Guide

> Then the believers immediately sent Paul away to the coast, but Silas and Timothy remained behind.
>
> (Acts of the Apostles 17:14)

A band of enthusiastic followers accompanied Paul on his adventurous preaching trips. Only a few names are recorded for us; Timothy's was one of them. Paul was often in controversy with some Jewish leaders and often led his companions into danger. They faced riots, shipwrecks, and even prison. When a young believing community sprang up in Beroea, Paul left Timothy and Silas behind to guide the new believers.

Because of Timothy's dedication, he was trusted with guiding others in the faith. When we are responsible and show dedication to the tasks assigned to us, others will feel confident in giving us new leadership roles.

How have you shown dedication to the responsibilities you have been given?

God, bless all who have been dedicated to guiding me, especially my parents, teachers, counselors, and coaches.

- To go deeper: Read Acts of the Apostles 17:10–15.

Timothy: Respected Pastor

> To Timothy, my loyal child in the faith: Grace, mercy, and peace from God the Father and Christ Jesus our Lord.

> (1 Timothy 1:2)

Evidence of Paul's respect for Timothy is preserved to this day in the two pastoral letters addressed to Timothy. The letters are guidelines for a good pastor and tell what to look for in a worthy bishop or deacon. They also talk about proper behavior for men and women in church. The letters express concern that good pastoral practices be observed, and they urge the people to pray for everyone, but especially for those in leadership positions.

The letters to Timothy can be summed up like this: A good leader is faithful to the Gospel message and has a clear conscience. In other words, a good leader sets an example for those who follow.

What do you consider proper behavior for a good leader?

Lord, strengthen and bless those in leadership roles in my parish, especially my pastor.

- To go deeper: Read 1 Timothy 3:1–13.

Timothy: Proclaimer of Truth

> I [Paul] solemnly urge you [Timothy]: proclaim the message; be persistent whether the time is favorable or unfavorable.
>
> (2 Timothy 4:1–2)

In the Second Letter to Timothy, Paul looked back over his missionary travels. Seeming to know his death was near, Paul encouraged Timothy to carry on the work Paul began. He reminded Timothy of all he had learned from Paul and from the Scriptures and to use his training to patiently, but persistently, bring others to Christ. Paul also warned Timothy that a time would come when people would not listen to the truth but only follow their desires.

Unfortunately, it is common today for people to ignore the truth if it interferes with their lifestyle. Some messages in the media and our culture suggest the truth is whatever we feel is right. But God's truth stays the same, no matter how we feel.

When has following the truth interfered with what you wanted?

Dear God, help me follow and speak the truth as Timothy did.

- To go deeper: Read 2 Timothy 3:10—4:8.

Silas: Belief and Ritual

> Judas and Silas, who were themselves prophets, said much to encourage and strengthen believers.
>
> (Acts of the Apostles 15:32)

Silas was another brave disciple who risked his life to accompany Paul on his journeys. Silas was chosen to go with Paul, Barnabas, and Judas to tell the Christians in Antioch the decision of the first Church council. There was confusion in the early Church about which of the Jewish laws should continue to be observed. Silas explained the new simplified rules and encouraged the fast-growing Christian community to remain strong in its faith.

The Council of Jerusalem was a turning point in Church history—the Apostles decided that Gentile Christians did not have to follow all the Jewish rituals. Belief in the risen Christ was more important than ritual.

Are there any Church rituals you do not understand? What can you do to understand them better?

God, help me appreciate the rituals of my faith and remember that they point to you.

• To go deeper: Read Acts of the Apostles 15:22–35.

Silas: Patient Endurance

The crowd joined in attacking [Paul and Silas].

(Acts of the Apostles 16:22)

After a disagreement with Barnabas, Paul decided to take Silas with him on a return visit to the Christian communities he had founded. Paul and Silas faced many inconveniences and dangers during their journey. Primitive methods of travel and uncertain passage meant hours or days of waiting, unscheduled stops, and detours. And then there were the angry mobs that beat them and threw them in jail. Silas had to have been a man of great patience to endure such trials.

We live in an instant culture. We want everything right now and the way we like it. We want fast food, instant relief from any and all pain, and we don't want to wait in line or traffic. We could learn a lot from Silas.

How can you be more patient? What sufferings are you called to endure?

God, help me slow down and be more patient with myself and with others.

- To go deeper: Read Acts of the Apostles 15:36 — 16:24.

Silas: Set Free

> Then the [jailer] brought [Paul and Silas] outside and said, "Sirs, what must I do to be saved?"
>
> (Acts of the Apostles 16:27)

While Paul and Silas were in Philippi, they were beaten, arrested, and thrown into prison. At midnight, as the two prisoners prayed, there was an earthquake. All the prison chains were shaken loose, and the doors to the jail cells were opened. The jailer, sure the prisoners had escaped, was about to kill himself when Paul and Silas told him not to harm himself. Struck by the fearlessness of Paul and Silas and their faith in God, the jailer asked how he could be saved. Their response—just believe in the Lord and you will be saved.

The jailer recognized that it was really he who needed to be set free, not Paul and Silas. We often see what imprisons others but fail to see what is keeping us from being truly free.

What do you need to be set free from in your life?

Savior God, help me recognize your saving action in my life.

• To go deeper: Read Acts of the Apostles 16:25–40.

Thomas: The Twin

> Thomas, who was called the Twin, said to his fellow disciples, "Let us also go, that we may die with him."
>
> (John 11:16)

The Gospels never tell us who Thomas's twin is. Some scholars speculate the twin is human nature. Throughout the Gospels, Thomas voices what we feel, struggle with, and believe. Jesus's dear friend Lazarus had died, and Jesus had told his disciples they needed to go be with Lazarus. Similarly, in great boldness and conviction, Thomas urged his fellow disciples to make the journey into hostile territory so they too could die with the Lord.

Many young people believe they can conquer the world and are invincible. This sense of confidence certainly explains Thomas's dedication to the Lord. We might ask ourselves if we have the passion and desire to live and die for the Lord as Thomas did.

When have you felt like you could do anything the Lord might ask of you?

God, give me the desire to follow you wherever you might lead me.

- To go deeper: Read John 11:1–16.

Thomas: Show Me the Way

> Thomas said to him, "Lord, we do not know where you are going. How can we know the way?"

> (John 14:5)

On the journey of life, one of our greatest needs is to know what we don't know. People who think they know it all rarely do and thus can be dangerous to fellow travelers. Thomas, one of the twelve Apostles, would be a welcomed companion to anyone traveling through life. He asked questions; he wasn't afraid to admit he didn't know everything.

The question Thomas asked Jesus is essential to following Jesus and finding our way through life. It would seem that Thomas had a definite advantage because he was speaking directly to the Lord. Yet anyone seeking to follow Jesus can turn to him in prayer. Prayer does not have to be formal; it just needs to be from the heart. The concerns, questions, and hopes the heart holds are what God hears.

What are the concerns and questions you have for the Lord?

May the questions of my heart, Lord, guide me in following your way.

- To go deeper: Read John 14:1–14.

Thomas: Count Me In

> Simon Peter said to [Thomas and the other disciples],
> "I am going fishing." They said to him, "We will go
> with you."
>
> (John 21:3)

Out of despair, disappointment, and discouragement,
some of the disciples returned to an old pastime—fishing.
Thomas was a part of this angler group. During times of
struggle, being with others is important. Being alone can
lead to isolation and depression. Thomas desired to be
with his buddies as they spent the night fishing. When
morning came, they discovered the Lord waiting for them
on shore, ready to fix breakfast.

It is not uncommon for young people to seek support by
gathering in groups. When life feels heavy, having friends
to be with provides us with an opportunity to share the
burdens of life. Shared interests and common experiences
can lighten our hearts and bring hope.

How are you and your friends supportive of one
another?

*Gracious God, gather my friends and me into a
supportive group of care and concern.*

• To go deeper: Read John 21:1–14.

Thomas: I Doubt It

> [Thomas] said to them, "Unless I see the mark of
> the nails in his hands, and put my finger in the
> mark of the nails and my hand in his side, I will not
> believe."
>
> (John 20:25)

Thomas would be right at home in our world, where
doubting is typical and trust is almost nonexistent. Thomas
wanted to see and feel Christ; only then would he believe.
He would not take anyone's word that they had seen the
risen Lord. Christ fulfilled Thomas's wish when he appeared
to him and invited him to touch, see, and believe.

Young people are often filled with questions, struggles,
and doubts as they seek to develop a relationship with the
Lord. Like Thomas, you need to integrate what you can
see and feel with those mysteries that are accepted on the
basis of belief in Christ. Questioning is necessary in the
process of believing.

What are the most common doubts you struggle with?

*My Lord and my God, when doubts abound, may
your grace lead me to belief in you.*

• To go deeper: Read John 20:24–29.

James: Answering God's Call

[James and his brother John] left their father Zebedee in the boat with the hired men, and followed [Jesus].

(Mark 1:20)

Imagine you and your dad are washing, waxing, and polishing your first car. That car is your way to work and to a social life. You have spent long hours working to afford it; it is your prized possession. Along comes a stranger who invites you to follow him, and off you go, leaving the car and your father behind.

That is precisely what happened to James when Jesus chose him to be one of the Twelve. The story has an air of urgency and disbelief about it, and yet we know it is true. We also know that Jesus's presence was, and is, so attracting that many do extravagant things to answer Christ's call.

How is the Lord calling you to serve God's people? Could it be as a priest, religious, deacon, or lay ecclesial minister?

Christ who calls us each to serve, help me hear your voice and answer your invitation.

• To go deeper: Read Mark 1:16–20.

James: Burning with Anger

> When his disciples James and John saw it, they said, "Lord, do you want us to command fire to come down from heaven and consume them?"
>
> (Luke 9:54)

Your face feels and looks like it is on fire, your muscles are taut, your mouth is dry, and you want to lash out verbally and physically. You have just been rejected, left out, and turned away. You're burning with anger, and you want fire to consume those who have hurt you. That's how James and his brother John felt when a Samaritan village did not receive Jesus and his disciples.

We all experience feelings of anger at being slighted or rejected. Despite James's anger, he was wise enough to stop and ask Jesus what he wanted done before he struck out against the village. Jesus makes known that retaliation is not the answer, and with that we must move on.

In moments of anger, do you stop and ask God how you should respond before acting?

God, fill my heart with your calming presence when I experience the heat of anger.

- To go deeper: Read Luke 9:51–56.

James: A Mountaintop Moment

> Six days later, Jesus took with him Peter and James and John, and led them up a high mountain apart, by themselves.
>
> (Mark 9:2)

Mountains have often been seen as places to meet God. Mountaintop experiences—where humans become more aware of God—are common to most religions. James was privileged to know just such a moment, a moment of solitude and connection with the Lord as Jesus's glory was revealed. Jesus knew that being away from the crowds and the demands of everyday life were necessary for encountering God at a deeper level.

Retreats, days of reflection, and times of solitude are often opportunities for us to get away and become more aware of God's presence in our lives. Taking time away from the routine of daily life in order to get a glimpse of the divine sustains our lives as followers of Christ.

When have you had a mountaintop experience with God?

God, bring me to the mountain of your presence where I may see your glory.

• To go deeper: Read Mark 9:2–8.

Priscilla and Aquila: Leaders in the Early Church

> Paul went to see [Priscilla and Aquila], and . . . he stayed with them.
>
> (Acts of the Apostles 18:2–3)

Priscilla and Aquila, a married couple, were leaders in the early Church. They extended hospitality to Paul not only by having him stay with them but also by using their home as a place for the Church to gather. House churches were places where the early Christians gathered to hear the word of Jesus, to share fellowship, and to break bread in sharing the Eucharist.

Missionaries like Paul depended on the generosity of the early Christian communities for support. Recorded accounts indicate it was an honor to have the traveling preachers stay at one's home. We are enriched when we take time to welcome people from outside our local community.

When have you heard someone preach from outside your own local church? What message did the person share?

God, let me always offer hospitality to others, especially those in need.

- To go deeper: Read Acts of the Apostles 2:43–47.

Priscilla and Aquila: Examples of Generosity

> Paul left Athens and went to Corinth. There he found a Jew named Aquila . . . with his wife Priscilla.
>
> (Acts of the Apostles 18:1–2)

Priscilla and Aquila had recently moved to Corinth from Rome, where the Emperor Claudius had expelled all Jews. Like Paul, Aquila and Priscilla were tent makers. When Paul lived with them in Corinth, the three of them worked together making tents, and they became good friends. Priscilla's and Aquila's support of Paul was instrumental in helping the early Church grow.

Priscilla and Aquila offered both their home and their treasure in support of Paul's ministry. We also have the opportunity to spread Jesus's message today by sharing our talents and financial resources with our parish.

What talents do you have that could be used in the ministries in your parish?

God, help me seek out ways to use my gifts and talents in your Church.

• To go deeper: Read Acts of the Apostles 18:1–4.

Priscilla and Aquila: Holy People

> Paul said farewell to the believers and sailed for Syria, accompanied by Priscilla and Aquila.
>
> (Acts of the Apostles 18:18)

Paul brought Aquila and Priscilla to Ephesus to be the leaders of the Christian Church there. After training them in Corinth, Paul had full confidence they would lead the Church wisely, so he left Priscilla and Aquila in charge when he traveled to other places. Paul's opening words in the Letter to the Ephesians tells of their success: "To the saints who are in Ephesus and are faithful in Christ Jesus" (1:1).

Priscilla and Aquila did not hold any official title of leadership, but they generously provided the Church leadership in how to grow in holiness. Every baptized Christian is called to live a life of holiness and to bring others to holiness as well.

How has your personal holiness inspired your friends to be holy?

God, help me grow in holiness so I am able to light the path for others.

• To go deeper: Read Acts of the Apostles 18:18–23.

Priscilla and Aquila: Quality Teachers

When Priscilla and Aquila heard [Apollos], they took him aside and explained the Way of God to him more accurately.

(Acts of the Apostles 18:26)

In First Corinthians, chapter 12, Paul talks about the many gifts found in the Body of Christ, the Church. One particular gift is that of teaching. Priscilla and Aquila were excellent teachers. They instructed Apollos, a Scripture scholar in his own right, in the faith so that he came to a fuller understanding of Jesus.

The gifts Paul refers to are wisdom, knowledge, faith, healing, miracles, prophecy, discernment of spirits, and speaking in and interpreting tongues. The Church believes different members are given different gifts by the Holy Spirit with the purpose of building up the Church.

What gifts of the Holy Spirit have been given to you? How do you use your gifts to better the Church community?

God, may I use the gifts you have given me for the good of all.

- To go deeper: Read Acts of the Apostles 18:24–28.

Philip: One of the First Deacons

[The Community] chose Stephen . . . Philip, Prochorus, Nicanor, Timon, Parmenas, and Nicolaus. . . . They had these men stand before the apostles.

(Acts of the Apostles 6:5–6)

Philip, not to be confused with Philip the Apostle, was chosen from among a group of disciples to serve the Greek-speaking community that had converted to Christianity. Philip was chosen by the community because the Holy Spirit's presence was evident in his works of faith. As Philip cared for the needs of the community members, he also preached the Gospel of Jesus Christ in a language his peers could understand.

Through everyday acts of kindness in caring for your peers, you make present the Holy Spirit of God. By serving others and proclaiming God's word, you enflesh the Good News of Jesus Christ in a way your peers can understand.

How do you proclaim the Gospel in a way that speaks to your peers?

God, help me serve your people, especially my peers, through kind acts of faith.

• To go deeper: Read Acts of the Apostles 6:1–7.

Philip: Evangelizer

> Philip went down to the city of Samaria and proclaimed the Messiah to them.

> (Acts of the Apostles 8:5)

Because of the intensity of the persecution of Christians in Jerusalem, Philip was led by God to Samaria to preach the Gospel message. The Samaritans were also awaiting the Messiah. Through Philip's words and miraculous works done in Jesus's name, many Samaritans discovered that Jesus was the long-awaited Messiah and were converted and baptized. This group of Samaritans, once excluded from Judaism, was now welcomed into the expanding Christian Church.

Many people, even today, are waiting to hear the Good News. They long to know the spiritual freedom Jesus brings. Jesus breaks down the barriers that keep individuals disconnected from the larger community.

How can you reach out to those who are excluded in our culture?

God, lead me to those who are in need of hearing the liberating message of your Son, Jesus.

- To go deeper: Read Acts of the Apostles 8:4–13.

Philip: Ethiopian Encounter

Philip and the [Ethiopian], went down into the water, and Philip baptized him.

(Acts of the Apostles 8:37–38)

When Philip encountered the Ethiopian, he was reading aloud from the Book of Isaiah. The man was familiar with Judaism because he was returning from worship in Jerusalem. As Philip interpreted the reading from Isaiah, the Ethiopian came to understand the Good News of Jesus and recognized that he was invited to become a follower of Christ. The Ethiopian was baptized immediately; thus, Christianity spread to Africa.

Each of us has an opportunity to help others understand how Jesus is inviting them to be a part of the Church. In listening to and trying to understand their struggles, we may be able to help them see Jesus and grow in faith.

How have you helped others deepen their faith through the word of God?

God, give me the wisdom to help others to read, understand, and respond to your word.

• To go deeper: Read Acts of the Apostles 8:26–40.

Man Born Blind: Overcoming Darkness

> Then [the blind man] went and washed and came back able to see.
>
> (John 9:5)

The Gospel of John returns often to the theme of light and darkness. This theme is played out dramatically when a man who was born blind received his sight after following Jesus's instructions. Jesus took mud made from his saliva and dirt (both symbols of darkness) and spread that mud on the blind man's eyes. He sent the man to the pool of Siloam to wash, and when the man came back, he was able to see. Darkness was overcome with light.

The blindness most of us experience is not the loss of eyesight, but the darkness that keeps us from seeing God's goodness in the world. Our culture and the news media place so much attention on the negative things in our society that we can become blind to the noble and good things people are capable of.

When have someone else's good deeds inspired you to do something good?

Lord of Light, wash away the darkness that keeps me from seeing your goodness.

- To go deeper: Read John 9:1–12.

Man Born Blind: Beyond Outward Appearances

> So [the Pharisees] said again to the blind man, "What do you say about him?" . . . [The man who had been blind] said, "He is a prophet."
>
> (John 9:17)

The Pharisees questioned the man as to how he, a man born blind, could now see. When the man said it was Jesus who gave him his sight, the Pharisees claimed Jesus could not be from God because he disregarded Jewish Law by healing the man on the Sabbath. When asked who he thought Jesus was, the man correctly identified Jesus as a prophet, for he had shown the way to God more clearly than any Sabbath observance.

Jesus is the great window to God; he leads us to see the goodness of God within each person. God's law does not exist to condemn us, but to point us to Jesus, who does not judge by outward appearances but sees what is in the human heart.

When have you let someone's outward appearance keep you from recognizing Christ in them?

Lord, help me see with your eyes of love.

• To go deeper: Read John 9:13–17.

Man Born Blind: Seeing Clearly

> [The man who had been blind] answered, ". . .
> One thing I do know, that though I was blind, now
> I see."
>
> (John 9:25)

The Pharisees kept questioning the man, hoping he would admit that Jesus was a sinner and could not have given him sight. The man refused to get into a debate with them and would only admit to what he knew—he was blind but now he could see. The honest answers of the man confused the issue even more, as he asked how those who had been disciples of Moses could not recognize the work of God.

The irony in this story is that the man who was born blind could see, but those born with sight could not see. The man born blind was open to changing and seeing in a new way; the Pharisees and Jews were not. They held to their beliefs despite the evidence before them.

When have you believed something to be true when evidence told you otherwise?

Lord of all sight, help me see clearly.

• To go deeper: Read John 9:18–34.

Man Born Blind: Believing

[The man who had been blind] said, "Lord, I believe."

(John 9:38)

After the man born blind was cast out by those who questioned him, Jesus sought out the man before he even had a chance to go looking for Jesus. The story ends with the now-seeing man able to look upon Jesus and proclaim him as the Messiah.

The man born blind did not immediately recognize Jesus as the Messiah when he received his sight, but came to understand Jesus's identity gradually. Our faith and relationship with Jesus develops in the same way. It is first Jesus who seeks us out, and if we are open to seeing Jesus, we will gradually come to recognize him in our lives.

How have you grown in your understanding of Jesus since you were a child?

Lord, help me believe you are present in my life even when I fail to recognize you.

• To go deeper: Read John 9:35–41.

Simon of Cyrene: Taking Up the Cross

> As they went out, they came upon a man from
> Cyrene named Simon; [the soldiers] compelled this
> man to carry [Jesus's] cross.
>
> (Matthew 27:32)

Simon (or "Rock") of Cyrene has become for Christians
a symbol of help during Jesus's darkest hour, the final
moments of his life. It appears that Simon was just passing
by when the soldiers grabbed him and pressed him into
carrying Jesus's cross. Jesus, already having been beaten
and tortured, was beginning to lose quite a bit of blood.
Simon did not appear to resist, but took up the long
crossbeam and moved the procession to the inevitable,
the Crucifixion of the Lord.

At some time in our lives, each of us will be asked to
take on an unpleasant task or to do something we would
rather not do. Simon can serve as an example of how to
take up the cross and carry it patiently.

Who do you know is in need of help?

*Lord, teach me to respond to opportunities to serve
with a willing spirit.*

• To go deeper: Read Matthew 27:24–37.

Simon of Cyrene: Carrying Another's Burden

"Take my yoke upon you, and learn from me; for I am gentle and humble in heart, and you will find rest for your souls."

(Matthew 11:29)

Though Simon probably didn't know Jesus, he may have heard of the rabbi from Nazareth. When he encountered Jesus, Jesus was near collapse and the soldiers were anxious to carry out the sentence of death by crucifixion before the Sabbath began. This Jesus who had offered to relieve the load of all those who were weary now needed someone to take the load off his shoulders. Simon willingly offered his shoulder to hoist and carry Jesus's burden.

The irony is that in helping others it is often we that are really helped. Helping to ease another person's burdens gives us a deep sense of peace within and increases our compassion for the suffering of others.

When have you lightened the load of another by offering to help?

God, make me gentle and humble of heart and willing to carry the burden of another.

• To go deeper: Read Matthew 11:25–30.

Simon of Cyrene: Witnessing the Messiah

"Truly this man was God's Son."

(Matthew 27:54)

Not much is written about Simon, but one wonders if Simon stayed around to witness Jesus's execution and death on the cross. Jesus, with a sign over his head proclaiming him King of the Jews, was the first to die of the three men who were executed that day. As the sky darkened and Jesus breathed his last, the roll of an earthquake bounced stones and boulders to and fro. Those who witnessed all this acknowledged that Jesus truly must be God's Son.

Simon most likely knew very little about Jesus when he was first asked to carry Jesus's cross. But if he had stayed around long enough, he would have been among those who had grown to understand that Jesus was the Messiah, the one sent to save us from our sins.

Have you helped someone without knowing who that person was?

Lord, help me see that in helping others, even strangers, it is you I am helping.

• To go deeper: Read Matthew 27:32–54.

Barnabas: Assistant to the Apostles

> There was a Levite . . . to whom the apostles gave the name Barnabas (which means "son of encouragement").
>
> (Acts of the Apostles 4:36)

As a Levite, Barnabas belonged to a group that assisted the Jewish priests by purifying holy things, preparing bread, and taking care of the sanctuary. After becoming a believer, Barnabas was appointed as an assistant to the Apostles and given the name "son of encouragement." Even though Barnabas was not a priest or an Apostle, he radiated encouragement to all he met.

For some people, if they can't be first or the best, then they don't want to participate. Somehow being an assistant seems beneath them. Barnabas shows us how a dedicated assistant can bring hope and encouragement to all.

How do you feel about assisting others?

God, help me serve you lovingly, even when I am called to be an assistant.

- To go deeper: Read Acts of the Apostles 4:32–37.

Barnabas: The Joy of Giving

> [Barnabas] sold a field that belonged to him, then brought the money, and laid it at the apostles' feet.
>
> (Acts of the Apostles 4:37)

"It's mine" and "I had it first" are two phrases we hear far too often in our culture today. Not only do we jealously hold on to possessions, we also seek to acquire more and more of them. Barnabas was just the opposite. He took what was his, sold it, and gave the proceeds to the apostles to use for the needs of the church. Barnabas was so detached from material goods that he even sold his property to support the work of the apostles.

As our sense of self-worth develops, it is easy to fall into the trap of identifying who we are with what we have and own. Getting the latest and the greatest becomes more important than sharing with those in need. Barnabas teaches us that true greatness lies in what we give not in what we get.

When have you known the joy of giving rather than getting?

Generous God, help me freely give what I possess to those in need.

- To go deeper: Read Acts of the Apostles 4:32— 5:11.

Barnabas: Apostle to the Apostles

> Barnabas took [Paul], brought him to the apostles, and described for them how on the road he had seen the Lord.
>
> (Acts of the Apostles 9:27)

Paul, having been converted from persecutor to proclaimer of the Gospel, was on his way to becoming an apostle to the Gentiles. Barnabas saw Paul's potential and was instrumental in convincing the apostles to accept Paul. When everyone else feared Paul's conversion as a ploy to arrest more Christians, Barnabas came to his defense. Barnabas trusted Paul's change of heart, stood by Paul when others opposed him, introduced Paul to the apostles, and verified Paul's story of conversion.

We also may be given the opportunity to support a friend who is trying to change. Support and encouragement are needed for conversion to take place, and friends like Barnabas can make all the difference.

When have you been a source of support and encouragement to a friend?

Lord, grace me with the ability to support and encourage others.

- To go deeper: Read Acts of the Apostles 9:1–31.

The Two Thieves: Jesus in Our Midst

> Then two bandits were crucified with him, one on his right and one on his left.
>
> (Matthew 27:38)

We know little about the two thieves. We know only that they, like Jesus, were condemned to death. Unlike Jesus, they were guilty. The term *bandit* meant that they were not only thieves but also that their crimes had been violent. The contrast is stunning. The bandits stole and brought chaos and pain; Jesus gave life and brought peace. In death as in life, Jesus excluded no one. His death was final testimony to the open and outstretched arms that typify Jesus's welcoming all.

We are no strangers to violence. Not only does it touch us personally, but we also witness everyday, through the media, the devastation violence causes. The two bandits surrounding Jesus at his death remind us that whatever life and death hold, the Lord is in our midst.

How has violence touched your life?

God, be at the center of my life, especially in times of chaos and loss.

• To go deeper: Read Matthew 27:32–44.

The Two Thieves: Biblical Bullies

> The bandits who were crucified with him also taunted him in the same way.
>
> (Matthew 27:44)

Children often steel themselves against the searing words of playmates with the verse, "Sticks and stones can break my bones, but names will never hurt me." And yet the verse doesn't deflect the pain. To be taunted is to feel one's self-confidence and self-worth called into question. Taunting is really the deadly art of bullying. The bandits crucified with Jesus were not the first bullies, nor were they the last. They provide a chance for us to reflect on the less than kind, and sometimes cruel, words we aim at others with the intention of inflicting pain. We are called to realize that the classmate we taunt or see taunted is loved and cherished by God as was Jesus, the Son of God.

What is your experience of being taunted or of taunting another?

God, keep me from launching hurtful words at others, and shelter me in your love.

- To go deeper: Read Matthew 27:32–44.

The Two Thieves: Guilty as Charged

"We are getting what we deserve for our deeds, but this man has done nothing wrong."

(Luke 23:41)

Human beings tend to want to avoid taking responsibility for their mistakes. It is much easier to blame someone else or claim that everyone else is doing it, so why shouldn't we. How different it was with the thief whom we now call "good." The good thief realized that he deserved his punishment but expressed faith in Jesus's compassionate mercy. His partner in crime, on the other hand, kept taunting Jesus and refused to believe in Jesus's saving power.

The teen years can be marked by poor choices and wrong turns. Admitting to being wrong and recognizing God's continued presence can change the direction of a young person's life. Knowing one is guilty is often the first step.

What has your experience been of admitting your guilt?

Forgiving God, remind me of your love and help me forgive myself.

- To go deeper: Read Luke 23:32–43.

The Two Thieves: Paradise Promised

"Jesus, remember me when you come into your kingdom."

(Luke 23:42)

Perhaps the good thief had encountered Jesus before. He might have heard Jesus speak of God's love for all people, or maybe he was standing in the shadows when Jesus saved the adulterous woman from death. We will never know. What we do know is that the thief's last words were not the desperate cry of a dying, sinful man, but the prayer of a person living in confident hope of God's mercy. Jesus's response assured the thief he would be with Jesus in paradise.

Young people often display either overconfidence or a lack of self-confidence when facing life's challenges. Having confidence that the Lord is there to guide us and not condemn us assures us of God's promise of eternal life.

When have you placed confidence in God's forgiveness and love for you?

God of my life, grant me confidence in your love and assurance of your presence.

- To go deeper: Read Luke 23:32–43.

John: Beloved Disciple

> [Jesus] saw two other brothers, James son of Zebedee and his brother John . . . and he called them.
>
> (Matthew 4:21)

John was a fisherman and worked with his brother, James, and their father, Zebedee. They made their home in the city of Capernaum, the same city where Peter lived. Jesus called John away from his father and his work as fisherman to follow him. The Gospels indicate that Jesus and John had a close friendship, and tradition places John at Jesus's side at significant junctures of Jesus's public life.

Most of us know the importance of having a best friend. She or he is the one who is always there for us—in both the good times and the bad times. Our friend is the one we can trust completely, a beloved companion on the journey of life.

Who is your best friend? What significant experiences have you shared?

God, I am grateful for the good friends you have placed in my life.

- To go deeper: Read Matthew 4:18–22.

John: Among the First Disciples

> [Jesus] went a little farther, he saw James son of Zebedee and his brother John. . . . Immediately he called them.
>
> (Mark 1:19–20)

In Mark's Gospel account, John was part of the first group of disciples Jesus called to follow him. Jesus was very direct when he asked the disciples to follow, and they responded by following immediately. There was no doubt that Jesus wanted John to share in his mission. John accepted Jesus's invitation and jumped in with both feet.

John's enthusiasm for this new, exciting, and dynamic ministry of Jesus of Nazareth is evident in his willingness to leave everything at a moment's notice to follow Jesus. We are also called to be a part of this exciting and dynamic ministry of Jesus in the ordinary moments of our daily lives.

What is your attitude about being asked to follow Jesus?

God, give me the enthusiasm I need to grow in my relationship with you.

• To go deeper: Read Mark 1:16–20.

John: Part of the Inner Circle

Jesus took with him Peter and John and James, and went up on the mountain to pray.

(Luke 9:28)

On three separate occasions, Jesus took John, Peter, and James with him to witness significant events—Jesus's raising Jairus's daughter back to life, Jesus's appearing with Moses and Elijah during his Transfiguration, and Jesus's praying to his heavenly Father just before his arrest in the garden at Gethsemane. Jesus invited these three trusted friends to accompany him so they could come to a deeper understanding of his true identity.

Often being part of a small group allows us the opportunity to get to know people on a deeper level than would be possible in a large group. Sharing experiences within a small group also allows us to make connections and gain insights that we might not attain alone.

When has being a part of a small group caused you to gain new insights into your experiences?

God, may my small-group experiences help me know and understand you better.

- To go deeper: Read Luke 9:28–36.

John: The Last Supper

One of [Jesus's] disciples—the one whom Jesus loved—was reclining next to him.

(John 13:22)

In Jesus's culture, people reclined at a table that was low to the ground to eat their meals. They would lean on one side with their legs extended out away from them. John's reclining next to Jesus seems to indicate something significant, otherwise why mention it? It could simply mean that Jesus and John had a special friendship and that they usually reclined next to each other at meals, or that Jesus had invited John to be next to him because Jesus knew it was their last meal together.

In our culture, the placement of guests at a table during formal occasions is predetermined by etiquette. However, when we gather informally with friends for a meal, everyone usually takes a place at random.

What occasion would cause you to invite a special friend to come and sit next to you at a meal?

God, let the meals with my family and friends be a reminder of your Last Supper.

• To go deeper: Read John 13:21–30.

John: At the Cross

> Then [Jesus] said to the disciple, "Here is your mother."
>
> (John 19:27)

Just before Jesus was about to die on the cross, his strongest desire was the love he had for his mother, to make sure she was cared for after his death. In entrusting John with the care of Mary, Jesus showed he had complete confidence that John would provide a home for his mother in a society where widows without children had no means to support themselves except by begging. John graciously accepted and fulfilled Jesus's request.

Our culture has other ways of providing for the physical needs of those who are without family. And yet we still have the homeless among us. It is important to make sure people have a place to stay and food to eat, but even more important, that they have people who love them.

What opportunities do you have to provide love and care for those people who are alone?

God, make clear to me those people who are alone and in need of my love and care.

• To go deeper: Read John 19:17–30.

John: At the Tomb

> The two were running together, but the other disciple outran Peter and reached the tomb first . . . but he did not go in.
>
> (John 20:4–5)

Tradition tells us that the other disciple was John and that he arrived at the tomb first because he was younger. After Peter arrived, both disciples entered the tomb together. All they found were the clothes used to wrap Jesus's body. The Gospel records John's reaction, "He saw and believed" (20:8). John's faith allowed him to see and understand that Jesus had risen from the dead.

John's knowledge and understanding of Jesus culminated in that one experience. What John saw proved that all Jesus had said was true, even that he would rise from the dead on the third day. At times in our lives, everything we know and understand comes together in a single moment of enlightenment—an aha! moment.

When have you seen and believed?

God, let me savor those aha! moments in my life when everything comes together.

• To go deeper: Read John 20:1–10.

John: Pillar of the Church

> When James and Cephas and John, who were acknowledged pillars, recognized the grace that had been given to me, they gave to Barnabas and me [Paul] the right hand of fellowship.
>
> (Galatians 2:9)

Paul recognized John as one of the pillars of faith in the early Christian community. John was highly regarded not only as one of the original disciples of Jesus but also for the guidance he gave the early Church through his teachings. Jesus's intimate relationship with John modeled for the Church the love Jesus has for all people.

A pillar is a critical piece of support in a structure that is essential for it to remain standing. Christmas is an opportune time to reflect on the pillars of faith in our lives, those who have been concrete examples of Jesus the Emmanuel—God with us.

Who are pillars of faith in your parish community?

God, thank you for those individuals who are pillars of faith in my life.

- To go deeper: Read Galatians 2:1–10.

Birth of Jesus of Nazareth: Light of the World

> The true light, which enlightens everyone, was coming into the world.
>
> (John 1:9)

The time leading up to Christmas is filled with anticipation. All wait in darkness for the coming of the light. Israel waited for the coming of the Messiah. Mary and Joseph waited for the birth of Jesus. We await Christ's Second Coming. It is no accident that Christmas is celebrated during the winter solstice, when we are moving out of the darkest time of the year toward longer daylight hours. John's Gospel begins not with a story of the birth of Christ but by acclaiming Jesus as the light of the world, the Word of God living among us.

Consumerism and holiday glitz often obscure the true meaning of Christmas. Rather than worrying about buying or receiving that perfect gift, let us keep in mind that Christ came to make God's love known to a world lost in the darkness of sin.

How are you making God's love known?

Jesus, help me let your light shine by giving of myself as you did.

- To go deeper: Read John 1:1–17.

Stephen: Powerful Witness

> Stephen, full of grace and power, did great wonders and signs among the people.
>
> (Acts of the Apostles 6:8)

Stephen was one of seven deacons chosen to serve the needs of the early Church. Stephen's powerful witness to the Gospel message angered the synagogue officials because he accused them of not keeping God's law and of persecuting God's prophets. Stephen was put to death for speaking the truth and standing up for his beliefs, making him the first martyr of the Church.

Individuals who stand up and challenge the status quo are not usually received with open arms, especially when they are speaking the truth. Archbishop Oscar Romero, Maura Clarke, Ita Ford, Dorothy Kazel, and Jean Donovan lost their lives when they challenged the status quo in El Salvador by speaking up for the poor.

Whom do you know that has challenged the status quo and suffered because of it?

Lord, may I be willing to sacrifice everything for the truth of the Gospel.

• To go deeper: Read Acts of the Apostles 6:8–15.

Stephen: Ancestors in Faith

And Stephen replied, "Brothers and fathers, listen to me."

(Acts of the Apostles 7:2)

Stephen's lengthy speech to the synagogue council outlined God's divine presence in the lives of those who bravely sacrificed their lives for their faith throughout the history of Israel. In his speech, Stephen referred to "our ancestors," including himself as a loyal Jew who now saw further evidence of a new development in the faith. Those who preach the message of Christ will be persecuted just as their ancestors in faith were persecuted for foretelling the coming Messiah.

We also walk in the footsteps of our ancestors who have set an example for us in how to live our faith with conviction. It might not always be in the dramatic style of Stephen, but even quiet conviction and faithful service can be the stuff of heroes.

Who is your hero in the faith?

Lord, send faith-filled youth leaders who will inspire me to live and practice my faith.

- To go deeper: Read Acts of the Apostles 7:1–51.

Stephen: The Power of Forgiveness

> Then [Stephen] knelt down and cried out in a loud voice, "Lord, do not hold this sin against them."
>
> (Acts of the Apostles 7:60)

Stephen's speech had infuriated the crowd, and they began to hurl rocks at him. Just as Jesus forgave those who crucified him, Stephen begged mercy for those who were stoning him to death. Stephen life's work was finished. He courageously witnessed Christ's message of love to the very end. Then sadly, as if to prove that violence only brings more violence, chapter 8 of Acts begins, "That day a severe persecution began against the church."

One needs only to look at the wars being fought in our world today to realize that violence breeds more violence. It takes those who are willing to forgive to break the cycle of violence. When enough people forgive, maybe then the wars will stop.

What one thing can you do to reduce anger and violence?

Lord Jesus, may our sins of violence dissolve with your gentle love.

- To go deeper: Read Acts of the Apostles 8:1–4.

Wise Men: Following the Light

Wise men from the East came to Jerusalem, asking, "Where is the child who has been born king of the Jews?"

(Matthew 2:1–2)

The rise or fall of world leaders is often a sign of significant changes about to take place. Some wise men certainly took notice when they saw signs in the heavens that a king had been born in Jerusalem. We are not exactly sure where the wise men came from, what their names were, or even how many of them there were. What we do know is that they were foreigners from the East who recognized the signs of the time—that the star they observed in the sky pointed to the birth of someone who would change the course of history—so they followed the light.

There are signs of Christ's presence in our world today. Like the wise men, we must recognize the signs and then be willing to follow the light.

What signs of Christ's presence do you see today?

God, give me the wisdom needed to follow the light of your presence shining today.

- To go deeper: Read Matthew 2:1–9.

Wise Men: Finding the Light

> When [the wise men] saw that the star had stopped,
> they were overwhelmed with joy.
>
> (Matthew 2:10)

The wise men's search took them south to Bethlehem. Again they followed the star until they reached the place where the child was with his mother. On seeing Jesus, they knelt down in worship and offered gifts fit for a royal messiah—gold because he was a king, frankincense because he was God's Son, and myrrh because he would die to save us. The wise men's search was over. They had, at long last, found what they had been seeking—salvation. Their response was complete joy.

People sometimes search their whole life and never find what they are looking for because they search in all the wrong places. We can be certain that if we let Christ be our guiding light, we will find our heart's desire.

What are you searching for? How is Christ your guide?

Jesus, let your love be my guiding light through life.

• To go deeper: Read Matthew 2:7–11.

Wise Men: Taking A Different Road

> Having been warned in a dream not to return to Herod, [the wise men] left for their own country by another road.
>
> (Matthew 2:12)

Chances are the wise men never knew of Herod's attempt to kill Jesus and of his massacre of boys under two years old. We are told that after being warned in a dream not to return to Herod, the wise men decided to take a different road home. Matthew's Gospel goes on to say that soon after the wise men left, Joseph too had a dream telling him to flee Herod's wrath and to take Jesus and his mother to Egypt, where they became refugees.

In encountering Christ, the light, the wise men could no longer stay on the same road they had been following. As Christians, we are also being told to turn from evil and take a different road—a path that leads away from death toward life.

How are you being called to take a different path than the one you are on?

Lord, I am a refugee in search of a better life with you. Guide me safely home.

• To go deeper: Read Matthew 2:12–18.

Acknowledgments

The scriptural quotations contained herein are from the New Revised Standard Version of the Bible, Catholic Edition. Copyright © 1993 and 1989 by the Division of Christian Education of the National Council of the Churches of Christ in the United States of America. All rights reserved.

The scriptural quotation marked NAB is from the New American Bible with Revised New Testament and Revised Psalms. Copyright © 1991, 1986, and 1970 by the Confraternity of Christian Doctrine, Washington, D.C. Used by the permission of the copyright owner. All rights reserved. No part of the New American Bible may be reproduced in any form without permission in writing from the copyright owner.

During this book's preparation, all citations, facts, figures, names, addresses, telephone numbers, Internet URLs, and other pieces of information cited within were verified for accuracy. The authors and Saint Mary's Press staff have made every attempt to reference current and valid sources, but we cannot guarantee the content of any source, and we are not responsible for any changes that may have occurred since our verification. If you find an error in, or have a question or concern about, any of the information or sources listed within, please contact Saint Mary's Press.

Index

Reflections for specific biblical people and/or Scripture passages can be located by turning to the calendar dates listed under the biblical character's name.

Isaiah

Jacob

James

Jeremiah

Jesus of Nazareth

Job

John

Jn 11:34–35   Sep 30

Jn 11:43–44   Oct 1

Lydia

Acts 16:14   Oct 20

Acts 16:15   Oct 21

Acts 16:15   Oct 22

Maccabees

1 Mc 2:20   July 30

1 Mc 2:50   July 31

1 Mc 4:56   Aug 1

1 Mc 9:30   Aug 2

2 Mc 7:1   Aug 4

2 Mc 12:44   Aug 5

Man Born Blind

Jn 9:5   Dec 4

Jn 9:17   Dec 5

Jn 9:25   Dec 6

Jn 9:38   Dec 7

Mary and Martha

Lk 10:38   Oct 2

Lk 10:40   Oct 3

Jn 11:2   Oct 4

Lk 10:41–42   Oct 5

Jn 11:3   Oct 6

Jn 11:21   Oct 7

Jn 11:40   Oct 8

Mary Magdalene

Lk 8:1–2   Oct 30

Mk 16:9   Oct 31

Jn 19:25   Nov 1

Mk 15:47   Nov 2

Mt 27:60–61   Nov 3

Mk 16:1   Nov 4

Jn 20:16   Nov 5

Mary of Nazareth

Lk 1:30   Aug 13

Lk 1:39   Aug 14

Rv 12:1–2   Aug 15

Lk 2:19   Aug 16

Jn 2:5   Aug 17

Lk 2:34–35   Aug 18

Jn 19:27   Aug 19

Micah

Am 5:24   June 4

Mi 3:1   June 8

Mi 5:2   June 9

Mi 6:8   June 10